Brander Matthews

Tom Paulding; the story of a search for buried treasure in the streets of New York

Brander Matthews

Tom Paulding; the story of a search for buried treasure in the streets of New York

ISBN/EAN: 9783743338890

Manufactured in Europe, USA, Canada, Australia, Japa

Cover: Foto ©ninafisch / pixelio.de

Manufactured and distributed by brebook publishing software (www.brebook.com)

Brander Matthews

Tom Paulding; the story of a search for buried treasure in the streets of New York

TOM PAULDING

THE STORY OF A SEARCH FOR BURIED TREASURE
IN THE STREETS OF NEW YORK

BY
BRANDER MATTHEWS

NEW YORK
THE CENTURY CO.
1917

CONTENTS

		PAGE
I	THE SCENE OF THE STORY	1
II	AROUND THE BONFIRE	10
III	A WALK BY THE RIVER	21
IV	PAULINE AND THE CAREFUL KATIE	30
V	AT THE BREAKFAST-TABLE	40
VI	THE BOX OF PAPERS	51
VII	CAKES AND A COMPOSITION	68
VIII	A QUARREL AND AN ARRIVAL	77
IX	UNCLE DICK	87
X	A LESSON IN GEOGRAPHY	105
XI	SANTA CLAUS BRINGS A SUGGESTION	112
XII	THE FATE OF JEFFREY KERR	130
XIII	CHRISTMAS MORNING AND CHRISTMAS NIGHT	138
XIV	THE BATTLE OF THE CURLS	150
XV	A NEW-YEAR'S-DAY DEPARTURE	162

		PAGE
XVI	Tom has Patience	171
XVII	Enlisting Allies	181
XVIII	Making Ready	192
XIX	Jeffrey Kerr's Booty	204
XX	The "Working Hypothesis"	214
XXI	A Startling Discovery	226
XXII	Counsel	237
XXIII	Conclusion	245

ILLUSTRATIONS

	PAGE
THE STEALING OF THE TREASURE	FRONTISPIECE
SKETCH IN UPPER NEW YORK	4
TYPICAL SKETCHES OF UPPER NEW YORK	5
"TOM WAS TIED TO A STAKE, WITH HIS HANDS BEHIND HIM"	19
"TOM HAD MADE HER A SEAT ON ONE SIDE OF THIS TREE"	35
"'I'M GOING TO SEE IF WE CAN'T GET BACK SOME OF THAT STOLEN MONEY,' SAID TOM"	49
"TOM HAD TO PUZZLE OUT AND PIECE TOGETHER, BUT AT LAST HE GOT AT ALL THE FACTS SO FAR AS IT WAS POSSIBLE TO DISCOVER THEM"	57
"'GUESS WHAT I'VE FOUND!' SHE CRIED"	72
"TOM WAS ABLE TO FIND MOST OF THE POSITIONS INDICATED ON THE MAP"	83
PAULINE AND UNCLE DICK INSPECTING THE "CAT-RANCH"	89
UNCLE DICK TELLS TOM AND POLLY HIS ADVENTURES	97
UNCLE DICK TELLS POLLY ABOUT THE DIAMOND-FIELDS	109

	PAGE
Mr. Joshua Hoffmann has a Talk with Uncle Dick	115
"Corkscrew" Tells Uncle Dick and Tom of the Discovery by the Aqueduct Laborers	123
"'I Think I Know where the Thief is,' the Boy began"	131
Uncle Dick and Tom go to the Fire	146
"Involuntarily Tom Raised his Hand to his Head, and he felt the Little Twists of Paper"	159
"Tom would Pretend to Sound Rocks with a Stick"	175
"Tom said Solemnly, 'Fellows, can you Keep a Secret?'"	186
"Thus the Procession Set Out"	201
"In a Second he was Soaked Through"	212
"Tom Paulding Stooped and Picked Out a Dozen Yellow Coins"	215
"Taking up the Stopper, he Touched a Drop of the Liquid to the Marks"	235
"Tom Told her the Whole Story"	243
Mrs. Paulding Receives her Christmas Present	251

TOM PAULDING.

CHAPTER I.

THE SCENE OF THE STORY.

IN every great city there are unexplored fastnesses as little known to the world at large as is the heart of the Dark Continent. Now and again it happens that a sudden turn in the tide of business or of fashion brings into view these hitherto unexplored regions. Then there begins at once a struggle between the old and the new, between the conditions which obtained when that part of the city was ignored, and those which prevail now that it has been brought to the knowledge of men. The struggle is sharp, for a while; but the end is inevitable. The old cannot withstand the new; and in a brief space of time the unknown region wakes up, and there is a fresh life in all its streets; there is a tearing down, and there is a building up; and in a few months the place ceases to be old, although it has not yet become new.

During this state of transition there are many curious changes; and a pair of sharp eyes can see many curious things.

In this Manhattan Island of ours, there is more than one undiscovered country of this kind; and in a city as active and as restless as New York it is only a question of time how soon such a quarter shall be discovered, and rescued from neglect. Though a place may have been abandoned for a century, sooner or later some one will find it out again. Though it may have been left on one side during the forced march of improvement, sooner or later some one will see its advantages, and will make them plain.

At the time of this story, when our hero, young Tom Paulding, set forth upon his quest for buried treasure, in the ninth decade of the nineteenth century, the quarter of New York where he lived, and where he sought what had been lost more than a hundred years before, was passing through a period of transition. This part of New York lies above Central Park, behind Morningside Park and beside the Hudson River, where the Riverside Drive stretches itself out for two miles and more along the brow of the wooded hill.

This portion of the city has much natural beauty and not a little historic interest. Just beyond the rocky terrace of Morningside Park was fought the battle of Harlem Plains on September 16, 1776. Then it was that the British troops, having occupied the lower part of the island, assaulted the Continental forces, and were beaten back. For days thereafter, General Washington had his headquarters within a mile or two of the spot where General Grant now lies buried.

In the fourscore years which elapsed between the retirement of Washington from the presidency of these United States and the election of Grant to that exalted position, the part of Manhattan Island where Tom Paulding lived, and where his father, and his grandfather, and his great-grandfather had lived before him, changed very little. In 1876 it seemed almost as remote from the centers of trade and of fashion as it had been in 1776. Although it was not out of town, it was beyond the beaten track of traffic. Just before the Revolution, and immediately after it, handsome country-seats had been built here and there on the heights overlooking the Hudson. And here and there, on the rocky knobs that thrust themselves up through the soil, squatters had since set up their little wooden shanties, increasing in number as the edges of the city spread out nearer and nearer.

In time the Riverside Drive was laid out along the river; and then the transformation began. Day by day there were changes; and year by year the neighborhood was hardly recognizable.

Here had been one of the few spots on Manhattan Island where nature was allowed to run wild and to do as she thought best, unimpeded by man; and by great good fortune the advancing tide of city life was not allowed to overwhelm altogether the natural beauty of the region. The irregularities of the surface were planed over, it is true;

streets were cut through the walls of rock which then arose in jagged cliffs high above the sidewalks on both sides, and avenues were carried across sunken meadows, leaving deep, wide hollows where the winter snows collected.

Around the shanties which were perched upon the rocks, sheer above the new streets, goats browsed on the scanty herbage; and down in the hollows which lay below the level of the same thoroughfares, geese swam about placidly, and squawked when a passing boy was carelessly cruel enough to throw a stone at the peaceful flock.

SKETCH IN UPPER NEW YORK.

It is a region of contrasts as it is a time of transition. In one block can be seen the old orchard which girt about one of the handsome country-places built here early in the century; and in the next can be seen the frames of a market-gardener, who is raising lettuce under glass, on ground which the enterprising builder may demand any day. The patched and weather-stained shanty of the market-gardener may be within the shadow of a new marble mansion with its plate-glass conservatory. An old wooden house with a Grecian portico is torn down to make room for a tall flat,

TYPICAL SKETCHES OF UPPER NEW YORK.

stretching itself seven stories high, with accommodation for a dozen families at least. The builder is constantly at work. The insignificant whistle of his engine announces the morning; and the dull report of blasting is of daily frequency.

With its many possibilities, this is perhaps the part of New York where a boy can find the most wholesome fun. He is in the city, although he has many of the privileges of the country. He can walk under trees and climb hills; and yet he is not beyond the delights of the town. There are long slopes down which he may coast in winter; and there are as yet many vacant lots where he may play ball in summer. There is the Morningside Park with its towering battlements, just the place for a sham fight. There is the Riverside Park with its broad terrace extending nearly three miles along the river front, and with its strip of woodland sloping steeply to the railroad track by the river.

It is a place with nearly every advantage that a boy can wish. For one thing, there is unceasing variety. If he takes a walk by the parapet of the Riverside, the freight-trains on the railroad below rush past fiercely, and are so long that the engine will be quite out of sight before the caboose at the end comes into view. From the brow of the hill the moving panorama of the Hudson unrolls itself before him; above are the Palisades rising sheer from the water's edge and crowned with verdure; opposite is Weehawken, and just below are the Elysian Fields, now sadly shorn of their green beauty. No two views of the river are ever alike, except possibly in winter when the stream may freeze over. In the summer there is an incessant change; yachts tack across against the breeze; immense tows of canal-boats come down drawn by one broad and powerful steamboat; and pert little tugs puff their way up and down, here and there. The day-boats go up every morning and the night-boats follow them every evening. Excursions and picnic parties go by in double-decked barges, lashed together side by side, and gay with flags and music. Sometimes a swift steam-yacht speeds up stream to West Point, and sometimes a sloop loaded with brick from Haverstraw drifts down with the tide.

On land there is a change almost as incessant. Buildings are going up everywhere; shanties are being torn down; and streets are being cut through here and filled up there, and paved, and torn up again to lay pipe, and repaired again, and torn up yet once more. There is a constant effort toward the completion of the Riverside Park, and of Morningside Park but a few blocks beyond it. There is also the new aqueduct, bringing more water from the Croton hills to the host of dwellers in the city.

When Tom Paulding first saw the men at work on this great undertaking, he little knew how necessary that water would one day be to him in his quest, or how the laborers who were laying the gigantic pipes in deep trenches underground would unwittingly lend him their aid.

But there is no need to dally longer over this description of the place where the young New Yorker lived who is to be the chief character of the story set forth in the following pages. It is time now to introduce Tom Paulding himself;

to show you what manner of boy he was; to make you acquainted with his friends and companions; to explain how it happened that his uncle returned home in time to advise; and to tell how it was that he set out to find the treasure. What the final result of his quest was will be fully shown in this narrative; but whether or not Tom Paulding was successful in his endeavor, every reader must decide for himself.

CHAPTER II.

AROUND THE BONFIRE.

N one of the side streets extending eastward from the Riverside Park, a dozen boys were gathered about a barrel, which had been raised on four stones. It was late in the afternoon of the Tuesday following the first Monday in November; and the boys were about to exercise the immemorial privilege of young New Yorkers on election night. Between the stones which supported the barrel were two or three crumpled newspapers and a heap of shavings. Within the wooden chimney of the barrel itself were the sides of a broken box, six or eight short boards, and such other combustible odds and ends as the boys had been able to get together against the coming of the fiery holiday. The impromptu altar had been erected almost in the middle of the street; but as there was scarcely a house within a block on either side, and as few carriages or carts needed to come down that way, there was little danger that the bonfire of the "Black Band" would frighten any horses.

When the shavings had been inspected, and he had made sure that the flames would be able to rise readily through the improvised flue, the boy who seemed to be the leader looked around and said, "Who's got a match?"

"Here's a whole box!" cried little Jimmy Wigger, thrusting himself through the ring of youngsters ranged about the barrel. He was the smallest boy of all, and he was greatly pleased to be of service.

"Are you going to set it off now, Cissy?" a tall thin lad asked.

"Well, I am!" answered the boy who had been making ready for the fire. "We said that we'd start it up at five o'clock, did n't we?"

The speaker was a solidly built young fellow of about fourteen, with a round, good-natured face. His name was Marcus Cicero Smith; his father always called him "Cicero," and among his playfellows and companions he was known as "Cissy," for short.

A timid voice suggested, "What's your hurry, Cissy? Tom Paulding is n't here yet."

This voice belonged to Harry Zachary, a slim boy of scant thirteen, shy in manner and hesitating in speech. He had light golden hair and light-blue eyes.

"If Tom Paulding's late," replied Cissy, as he stooped forward and set fire to the paper and shavings, "so much the worse for Tom, that's all. He knows the appointed hour as well as we do."

"I'd just like to know what is keeping Tom. He's not

often late," said the tall thin lad who had spoken before, and as he said it he twisted himself about, looking over his shoulders with a strange spiral movement. It was partly on account of this peculiar habit of self-contortion that he was generally addressed as "Corkscrew." But that nickname had been given also because of his extraordinary inquisitiveness. His curiosity was unceasing and inordinate. It is to be recorded, moreover, that he had straight red hair, and that his thin legs were made more conspicuous by a large pair of boots, the tops of which rose above his knees. His real name was George William Lott.

As the wood in the barrel kindled and blazed up, the boys heaped on more fuel from a pile outside their circle. While taking a broken board from the stack, little Jimmy Wigger looked up and saw a figure approaching. The street where they were assembled had been cut through high rocks which towered up on each side, irregular and jagged. Twilight had begun to settle down on the city, and in the hollow where the roadway ran between the broken crags there was little light but that of the bonfire. It was difficult to make out a stranger until he was close upon them.

"Some one is coming!" cried little Jimmy, glad that he had again been able to be useful.

The approaching figure stood still at once.

The group about the fire spread open, and Cissy careened forward a few feet. He had always a strange swing in his walk, not unlike the rolling gait of a sailor.

When he had swung ahead four or five paces he paused

and raising his fingers to his lips, he gave a shrill whistle with a peculiar cadence:

The stranger also stood still, and made the expected answer with a flourish of its own:

"It's Tom Paulding," said Harry Zachary.

"I wonder what has made him so late," Corkscrew remarked.

Cissy Smith took another step forward, and cried, "Who goes there?"

The new-comer also advanced a step, which brought him into the glare of the blazing barrel. He was seen to be a well-knit boy of barely fourteen, with dark-brown eyes and curly black hair.

To Cissy's challenge he answered in a clear voice, "A friend of the Black Band."

"Advance, friend of the Black Band, and give the countersign and grip."

Each of the two boys took three paces forward, and stood face to face.

The new-comer bent forward and solemnly whispered in Cissy's ear the secret password of the Black Band, "Captain Kidd."

With the same solemnity, Cissy whispered back, "As he sailed." Then he extended his right hand.

Tom Paulding grasped this firmly in his own, slipping his little finger between Cissy's third and little fingers; then he pressed the back of Cissy's hand three times with his own thumb.

These proper formalities having been observed with due decorum, the boys released their grasp and walked together to the bonfire.

"What made you so late, Tom?" asked Corkscrew.

"My mother kept me while she finished a letter to my Uncle Dick that she wanted me to mail for her," Tom Paulding replied; "and besides I had to find my dark lantern."

"Have you got it here?" said Cissy.

"Oh, do let me see it!" cried little Jimmy Wigger.

Tom Paulding unbuttoned his jacket and took the lantern from his belt. There was at once perceptible a strong odor of burnt varnish; but the circle of admiring boys did not mind this. The possession of a dark lantern increased their admiration for its owner, who was a favorite, partly from his frank and pleasant manner, and partly because of his ingenuity in devising new sports. It was Tom Paulding who had started the Black Band, a society of thirteen boys all solemnly bound to secrecy and to be faithful, one to another, whatever might befall. Cissy Smith, as the oldest of the thirteen, had been elected captain, at Tom's suggestion, and Tom himself was lieutenant.

"Is it lighted?" little Jimmy Wigger asked, as he caught

sight of a faint spot of light at the back of the dark lantern in Tom's hand.

"Of course it is," Tom replied, and he turned the bull's-eye toward the rugged wall of rocks which arose at the side of the street, and pulled the slide. A faint disk of light appeared on the stones.

"That's bully!" said Harry Zachary, in his usual hesitating voice. "I wish I had one!"

"What good is a dark lantern, anyhow?" asked Corkscrew Lott, who was almost as envious as he was curious. "What did you bring it out for?"

"Well," Tom answered, "I had a reason. We had n't agreed what the Black Band was to be this evening; and I thought if we were burglars, for instance, it would be useful to have a dark lantern."

"Hooray!" said Cissy. "Let 's be burglars."

There was a general cry of assent to this proposition.

"A burglar always has a dark lantern," Tom went on, "and he 'most always has a jimmy—"

"Well, where 's your jimmy?" interrupted Lott.

"Here it is," Tom answered, taking a dark stick from its place of concealment in the back of his jacket. "It ought to be iron, you know; a jimmy 's a sort of baby crowbar. But I made this out of an old broomstick I got from our Katie. I whittled it down to the right shape at the end, and then I polished it off with blacking and a shoe-brush. It does look like iron, does n't it?"

The jimmy was passed from hand to hand, and met with

general approval. Even Corkscrew Lott had no fault to find with it.

"We ought to have everything real burglars have, if we are going into the burgling business," added Tom.

"If we are burglars," said little Jimmy Wigger, in a plaintive voice, "can't we begin burgling soon? Because my aunt says I must be home by eight this evening, sure."

"I said it was a mistake to let that baby into the Black Band," Corkscrew remarked; "a pretty burglar he'll make!"

"Yes, I will!" cried little Jimmy, sturdily; "I'll make as good a burglar as you any day!"

"I could tell you stories about burglars that would make your hair curl," said Harry Zachary, noticing that little Jimmy had shrunk back.

"Then tell them to Tom Paulding," Lott cried; "he likes to have his hair curl. I believe he puts it up in curl-papers!"

Now, if there was one thing which annoyed Tom more than another, it was that his hair was curly, "like a girl's" as he had said in disgust to his sister only that morning. And if there was any member of the Black Band toward whom he did not feel a brotherly cordiality, it was Lott.

"Look here, Corkscrew," he said hotly, "you let my hair alone, or I'll punch your head!"

"You had better not try it," returned Lott. "You could n't do it."

"We'll see about that, if you say anything more against my hair!" Tom replied.

"I'll say what I please," responded Corkscrew.

By this time Tom had recovered his temper.

"Say what you please," he answered, "and if it does n't please me, we'll have it out. The sooner we do, the better; for I don't believe we can get through the winter without a fight, and I sha'n't be sorry to have it over."

"Silence in the ranks," ordered the Captain of the Black Band, as he saw that Lott was ready to keep up the quarrel. "Is it agreed that we are to be burglars?"

"No," answered Corkscrew quickly, before any of the others could speak. "We have n't got all the things. Let's be Indians on the war-path. We've got a bully fire now and it's the only night we can have it. So we can play we've a captive, and we can burn him at the stake, and have a scalp-dance around the barrel."

"That's a good idea," Harry Zachary agreed. "They won't let us have a bonfire except on election night."

"That's so," Cissy admitted.

Lott saw his advantage and seized it promptly.

"We can be burglars any time," he cried, "if we want to. But to-night's the best time to be Indians. It's our only chance to burn a captive at the stake."

"We might make him run the gantlet first," suggested Harry Zachary, who was a delicate boy of a very mild appearance, but strangely fertile in sanguinary suggestions.

"Let little Jimmy Wigger be the captive," Lott proposed. "We won't hurt him much."

"No, you don't," Tom Paulding interposed. "Little Jimmy is too young. Besides, when his aunt let him join the Black Band, I promised that I would keep him out of mischief."

"Then who'll run the gantlet?" asked Lott, sulkily.

"I will," Tom answered. "I'd just as lief. In fact, I'd liefer. I've never been burned at the stake yet, and the Sioux shall see how a Pawnee can die!"

Then, at the command of Cissy Smith, the Black Band formed in a double row facing inward, and Tom Paulding ran the gantlet. When he came to the end of the lines he broke away, and the whole troop pursued him. After a sharp run he was caught, and brought back to the bonfire. More fuel was heaped upon this, and it blazed up fiercely. A stake was driven into the ground not far from the fire, and Tom was tied to it, with his hands behind him. Then, under the leadership of Cissy Smith, the Black Band circled about the fire and the stake, with Indian yells and shrill whistles. As the flames rose and fell on the shouting boys and on the broken rocks which towered high above them on both sides, an imaginative spectator might almost have fancied himself gazing at some strange rite of the redskins in a far cañon of Colorado.

"TOM WAS TIED TO A STAKE, WITH HIS HANDS BEHIND HIM."

CHAPTER III.

A WALK BY THE RIVER.

ABOUT six o'clock Jimmy Wigger's aunt came for him. He begged hard for only a few minutes more, but she did not yield and he went away reluctantly. Other members of the Black Band remembered that their suppers would be waiting for them; and soon the assembly broke up. The smaller boys were the first to go, and the Captain and Lieutenant of the Black Band were the last to leave the blazing barrel which now was almost burnt out.

Tom Paulding had released himself from the bonds that bound him to the stake; and as he was stooping over the embers to warm his hands, Cissy Smith proposed that they should go for a walk through the woods between the Riverside Drive and the river. Tom agreed at once, and asked Harry Zachary to come also.

Corkscrew Lott had started off ahead of them, but at the first corner he, too, joined the group.

The boys walked down the street four abreast, Cissy rolling

along irregularly in his usual fashion. They crossed the Riverside Drive and stood for a minute at the head of the stone steps that led to the strip of steep woodland below. There was a sharp whistle in the distance, and then an advancing roar; and a short passenger train rushed rapidly past them, the flying white steam from the engine reddened by the glare from the furnace as the fireman threw in fresh fuel. Out on the broad river beyond, one of the night-boats went up the river, its rippling wake gleaming in the bluish moonlight.

"I wonder why little Jimmy's aunt came for him so early," said Corkscrew, twisting himself up on the parapet to get a good look over it.

"If she 'd found him tied to the stake, and the Black Band scalp-dancing all around him, she 'd have been 'most scared out of a year's growth, I reckon," Harry Zachary commented. His mother was a Kentuckian, and it was from her that he learned his gentle ways and his excellent manners. He had taken also from her an occasional Southern phrase not common in New York.

"I don't believe it would be much fun to be an Indian really," Cissy remarked. "I guess they have a pretty hard time of it when it 's cold and rainy—leastwise those I 've seen West did n't seem any too set up and happy." Cissy's father, Dr. Smith, had only a short time before removed to New York from Denver.

"Have you seen real Indians out West?" asked Tom Paulding. "Were they on the war-path?"

"Not much they were n't. They were coming into the agency to get their rations," Cissy answered.

"Did you kill any of 'em when you had the chance?" asked Harry in his usual timid voice.

"I did n't kill 'em. Of course not," Cissy responded. "Why should I?"

Tom Paulding was kindly by nature, but he was a little disappointed to learn that his friend had neglected a chance to kill a redskin.

"Perhaps you 've never read a book called 'Nick of the Woods'?" Harry Zachary inquired. "That tells all about a man they called the Jibbenainosay, who lived in the forest and killed Indians, and marked every man he killed so that they should know the handiwork of the Mysterious Avenger."

"My Uncle Dick, when he went up to the Black Hills, had a fight with the Indians," said Tom.

"How many did *he* kill?" asked Corkscrew, promptly.

"He did n't know," replied Tom, "but—"

"If he did n't know how many he killed what was the use of talking about it?" Harry Zachary asked. "That is n't any way to do. The best plan is to be alone in the woods, and take 'em by surprise, and kill 'em, one by one, and mark 'em."

"And suppose one of them takes you by surprise and kills you, what then?" Cissy interposed.

"I reckon I 'd have to take my chances, if I was an Avenger," Harry admitted. "But in the books they 'most always get the best of it."

"Let's go down to the water as we said we would," suggested Cissy.

"Look at that schooner," Tom cried, as they were going down the long stone stairway. "She's a beauty, and no mistake."

"That's the kind of a ship I'd have if I was a pirate like Lafitte," said Harry Zachary.

"How can you be a pirate now, when there are policemen everywhere?" asked Cissy, scornfully.

"I'd like to be a pirate some place where there are n't any policemen," Harry explained. "Down in Patagonia, or up in Greenland, or somewhere."

"They'd be sure to send a big frigate after you," said Tom Paulding; "they always do."

"Then I'd fight the frigate till the deck ran with blood," persisted Harry, with a tone of excitement in his gentle voice. "I'd nail the black flag to the mast; and if they got the better of us I'd fire the powder-magazine and blow up the whole boat — and that would surprise them, I reckon."

"It is n't the kind of surprise party *I* want," said Cissy emphatically, as the boys came to a halt among the trees near the railroad track by the edge of the river.

"How many pirates would there be on a boat like that?" inquired Lott.

"How many beans make five?" Cissy Smith answered sarcastically. "There's a Boston problem for you."

Lott had been born in Boston, and he had lived in New York less than a year.

"I wish I knew a place where a pirate had buried his treasure," he remarked, paying no attention to Smith's taunt.

"Now, there's another thing that's great fun," Harry interjected, "and that's hunting for buried treasure. I've read all about that in a story called 'The Gold Bug.' It's pretty interesting, I reckon, to dig under a tree with a skeleton or a skull on one branch, and to find thousands and thousands of guineas and doubloons and pieces-of-eight."

"Pieces of eight what?" asked Cissy.

"Pieces-of-eight — why, that's just the name they have for them. They're some kind of a coin, I reckon," replied Harry.

"Pieces of eight cents, very likely," Cissy returned. "I don't believe it's worth while wearing yourself out with hard labor just to dig up a few pieces of eight cents. And who would all these guineas and doubloons and pieces of eight cents belong to when you found 'em?"

"They'd belong to us, I reckon," answered Harry.

"And just suppose they did n't?" retorted Cissy.

"Suppose the rightful owner turned up," suggested Tom Paulding; "the man who had buried the money during the war, or the son of the man, or his grandson?"

Harry Zachary was a little taken aback at this. His manner, always gentle and shy, now seemed milder than ever.

"Well," he said at last, "I reckon I'd have the luck to find the treasure that belonged to our family — that had been hid by my father, maybe, or my grandfather."

"Shucks!" cried Cissy, forcibly. "Being a pirate where there's no police and finding buried treasure that belongs to you—I don't think that's so very exciting, do you?"

Harry Zachary felt that this was a home thrust, and he had no retort ready. Tom Paulding came to his rescue and gave a practical turn to the talk.

"There's a buried treasure belonging to us, somewhere," he said, conscious of the envy this remark would excite.

"Where is it?" asked Corkscrew, promptly.

"If he knew where it was, don't you suppose he'd hustle round and get it?" Cissy remarked.

"It is n't really buried treasure," explained Tom, "at least, we don't know whether it's buried or not, or what has become of it. You see, it's just a lot of money that was stolen from my great-grandfather during the Revolutionary War."

"I guess the great-grandchildren of the man that stole it have a better chance of getting it than you have," said Cissy.

"He did n't leave any family—he did n't leave any trace of himself, even," Tom replied. "He just disappeared, taking the money with him. He's never been seen or heard of since, so my mother told me."

"And I guess the money will never be seen or heard of, either," Cissy remarked.

"How much was it?" Corkscrew inquired.

"Oh, a lot!" Tom answered; "several thousand pounds—as much gold as a man could carry. He took all he could lift comfortably."

"What would you do with it, if you had it?" asked Corkscrew.

"I'd pay off the mortgage on our house," said Tom, promptly. "And I'd get lots of things for Pauline — my sister, you know; and instead of going into a store as I've got to do next winter, I'd study to be a mining engineer."

"I'd rather be a soldier," Harry Zachary declared. "What would you like to be, Cissy?"

"It does n't make any matter what I'd like to be," replied Cissy; "I know what I am going to be — and that's a doctor. Pa says that he'll need an assistant by the time I'm through the medical school, and he allows he can ring me in on his patients."

"I have n't made up my mind what I'd like to be," said Lott. "At first I thought I'd choose to be an expressman, because then I'd get inside all sorts of houses, and see how the people lived, and learn all sorts of things. But I've been thinking it might be more fun to be a detective, because then I could find out anything I wanted to know."

"I guess it would take the Astor Library to hold all you want to know, Corkscrew," said Cissy, pleasantly, as the boys began to retrace their steps up the hill; "but all you're likely to find out could be put in a copybook!"

Lott fell back a little and walked by the side of Harry Zachary.

"I wonder what makes Cissy Smith so pernickety," he said. "He's always poking fun at me."

"I would n't mind him now," responded Harry, consolingly,

"and when you are a detective you can find out something about him and arrest him."

This comforting suggestion helped to keep up Lott's spirits, although Smith made more than one other sarcastic remark as the four climbed the hillside together.

"I can't bear that Corkscrew," Cissy confessed to Tom in a whisper.

"Well," Tom answered, also in a whisper, "I don't know that I really like him, myself. But he's one of the Black Band now, and I suppose we must stand by him."

When the boys came out again on the high parapet of the Riverside Drive, it was time for them to go home. They went through the parting rites of the Black Band. Cissy extended his right hand and gave Tom the secret grip of the society, while Lott and Harry Zachary clasped their hands in the same mystic manner above Tom's and Cissy's.

Then Tom left them and went homeward. He lived with his mother and his sister in an old wooden house in a side street not far from the steps they had just ascended. The other three boys lived farther down along the Park.

When Tom reached the flight of wooden steps that rose from the sidewalk to the rocky terrace above, where his mother's house was, he stood still for a moment. Then he gave the same whistle with which Cissy had greeted him when he drew near the bonfire that afternoon:

From over the houses and the little hills which separated his home from Cissy's, he heard the answer:

' Then the Captain of the Black Band and the Lieutenant knew that all was well; and they went in and went to sleep with clear consciences.

The talk that evening had turned Tom's thoughts to a search for the stolen gold, and he dreamed of finding it in a cave like the one the Forty Thieves lived in. But in the middle of his desperate struggle with six ferocious robbers (one of whom had only one arm) there came a tap on his door, and he waked with a start.

CHAPTER IV.

PAULINE AND THE CAREFUL KATIE.

HE house in which Tom Paulding lived with his mother and sister had originally been a small farmhouse. It had been built just before the Revolution and by Tom's great-grandfather, the officer from whom the gold had been stolen. It was a square wooden house with gable-ends and with a door in the middle; there was a little porch before the door with a vine climbing by the white wooden pillars. Originally it had stood on a knoll, overlooking the broad acres of the farm as they sloped down to the river. When the streets were regularly laid out through that part of the city, making the upper portion of Manhattan Island as like as possible to a flat gridiron, a lower level was chosen than that of the house. The stony hill was cut through, and the house now stood high on a bluff, rising sheer and jagged above the sidewalk. A flight of wooden steps led from the street to the top of the knoll; and thence a short walk paved with well-worn flagstones stretched to the front door. The house had

been so planted on the hill that it might command the most agreeable view; but the streets had been driven past it rigidly at right angles to the avenues, and so the house was now "cater-cornered" across one end of a block.

In the century and a quarter since Nicholas Paulding had bought a farm and built him a house, the fortunes of his children and grandchildren had risen and fallen. He himself had been a paymaster in Washington's army; and after the Revolution he had prospered and enlarged his domain. But as he grew old he made an unfortunate use of his money, and when he died his estate was heavily involved. His son, Wyllys Paulding (Tom's grandfather), had done what he could to set in order the family affairs, but he died while yet a young man and before he had succeeded in putting their fortunes on a firm basis. Wyllys's son, Stuyvesant (Tom's father), struggled long and unavailingly. Like Wyllys and like Nicholas, Stuyvesant Paulding was an only child; and Tom Paulding so far carried out this tradition of the family that he was an only son and had but one sister.

Stuyvesant Paulding had died suddenly, when Tom was about five years old, leaving his widow and his children nothing but the house in which they lived and the insurance on his life. Bit by bit the farm had been sold to meet pressing debts, until at last there was left in the possession of Nicholas Paulding's grandson but a very small portion of the many acres Nicholas Paulding had owned—only the house and the three city lots across which it stood. And upon these lots and the house there was a mortgage, the interest on which Tom's mother often found it very hard to meet.

Tom's mother was a cheerful little woman; and she was glad that she had a roof over her head, and that she was able to bring up her children and give them an education. The roof over her head was stanch, and the old house was as sound as when it was built. Mrs. Paulding was very fond of her home, and she used to tell Tom and Pauline that they were perhaps the only boy and girl in all New York city with its million and a half of inhabitants, who had been born in a house built by their own great-grandfather.

The household was small; it consisted of Mrs. Paulding, Tom, his sister Pauline, and the Careful Katie.

Cissy Smith had once told Tom that Mrs. Paulding was "the nicest old lady in the world,"—and Tom had indignantly denied that his mother was old. Perhaps she was not old, but assuredly she was no longer young. She was a trim little woman with a trim little figure. Her dark-brown hair was turning gray under the widow's cap that she had worn ever since Tom's father died. She was good-natured and even-tempered; her children had never seen her angry, however they might try her; to them she was always cheery and she seemed always hopeful. As far as she might have power, the path of life should always be smooth before her children's feet.

Tom Paulding was the second member of the family; and he often looked forward to the time when he should be a man, that he might do something for his mother and for his sister.

Tom called his sister "Polly," but her name really was Pauline. She was nearly twelve years old, and she was rather short for her years; she kept hoping to be taller when she was older.

"How can I ever feel grown up, if I have n't grown any?" she once asked her mother.

She was rather pretty, and she had light-brown hair, which she wore down her back in a pigtail. To live in a house with a little spare ground about it was to her a constant delight. One of the two trees which Nicholas Paulding had planted before his door-step, an ample maple, now spread its branches almost over the porch; and to this tree Pauline had taken a great fancy when she was but a baby. She called it *her* tree; and she used to go out and talk to it and tell it her secrets. Tom had made her a seat on one side of this tree; and there she liked to sit with the cat and the kitten. She was very fond of cats, and she had generally a vagrant kitten or two, outcast and ragged, whom she was feeding and petting. With all animals she was friendly. The goats which browsed the rocks on which stood Mrs. Rafferty's shanty, two blocks above on Pauline's way to school, knew her and walked contentedly by her side; and the old horse which was always stationed before the shanty, attached to a decrepit cart labeled "Rafferty's Express," knew Polly and would affably eat the apple she took from her luncheon for him. The name of this old horse was "Daniel."

There was not an animal anywhere on the line of Pauline's daily walk to and from school that did not know her and love her.

The fourth member of the household, and in some respects the most important, was the Careful Katie. She was a robust, hearty Irishwoman who had been in Mrs. Paulding's service for years. She had come to the young couple when Tom's father and mother were first married, and she had remained with the family ever since. She had been Tom's nurse and then she had been Polly's nurse. Now, in their reduced circumstances, she was their only servant, strong enough to do anything and willing to do everything. She could cook excellently; she was indefatigable in housework and in the laundry; she was a good nurse in sickness; and she had even attempted to raise a few vegetables, chiefly potatoes and beans, in the little plot of ground on one side of the house. She was never tired and she was never cross. She was a "Household Treasure," so said Mrs. Paulding, who also wondered frequently how she could ever get on without her.

She had two defects only, and these in a measure neutralized each other. The first was that she thought she wished to go back to Ireland; and so she gave Mrs. Paulding warning and made ready to depart about once every six weeks. But she had never gone; and Mrs. Paulding was beginning to believe that she never would go. The second of her failings was that she was conscious of her long service, of her affection for Mrs. Paulding and for the two children, and of her fidelity; and so she had come to accept herself as one of

"TOM HAD MADE HER A SEAT ON ONE SIDE OF THIS TREE; AND THERE SHE LIKED TO SIT WITH THE CAT AND THE KITTEN."

the family and to believe that she was therefore authorized to rule the household with a rod of iron. She was so fond of them all that she insisted on their doing what she thought best for them, and not what they themselves might prefer. There were times when the Careful Katie carried things with so high a hand that Mrs. Paulding caught herself half wishing that the attraction of Ireland might prove potent enough to entice the child of Erin back to her native isle.

It remains to be recorded, moreover, that the Careful Katie was very superstitious. She accepted everything as a sign or a warning. She would never look over her left shoulder at the new moon. She was prompt to throw salt over her right shoulder, if by chance any were spilt while she was waiting at table. She declared that a ring at the bell at midnight, three nights running, foreboded a death in the family.

On the morning after election-day, the morning after the Black Band had made Tom Paulding run the gantlet, and had tied him to the stake, and had danced a scalp-dance about him while he bravely chanted his defiant death-song, the imitator of Hard-Heart and Uncas was late for breakfast.

Mrs. Paulding and Pauline were at table, and the Careful Katie had placed the coffee-pot before his mother and the plate of hot biscuit before his sister; and Tom's chair was ready for him, but he had not yet appeared.

"It 's late Master Tom is," remarked the Irish member of the family. "Will I call him?"

The Careful Katie was fond of hearing herself talk, and she was always ready to take part in the conversation at the dinner-table; but her use of the English language left something to be desired.

"Tom will be down in a minute," said Pauline; "I knocked on his door as I passed, and waked him up, and I kept on knocking till I heard him get out of bed, and then he threw a pillow at me down the stairs."

"An' who 's to be washin' that same pillow-case, I 'd like to know? It is n't yous that 'll do it—it 'll be me, I 'm thinkin'," said the Irishwoman.

"Katie," interposed Pauline, pausing in her breakfast, "if you were a good girl, a real good girl, you would bring 'Pussy' up and 'Bobby,' and let me give them their breakfast."

"An' where will I find Pussy? Bobby is quiet in the kitchen with his feet to the fire like a gentleman; but Pussy does be out all night," replied Katie, adding, "Ah, but there's the cat now, sittin' outside the window here as easy as you please."

"Then I 'll let her have her breakfast right away, if you will please excuse me, Mama," cried Pauline, rising from the table and pouring out a saucerful of milk.

She opened the window and called the cat, who came to the sill and stood expectant. When Pauline was about to set the saucer outside for Pussy to drink, the Careful Katie saw what she was doing and rushed across the room.

"Miss Polly," she screamed, "never be doin' that! It's main bad luck to pass vittles out o' the window to a Christian, let alone to a cat."

Mrs. Paulding looked up and smiled, and then quietly went on eating her breakfast.

"Pauline," she said, presently, "your own breakfast will be cold."

"But just see how hungry Pussy is," the little girl said as she came back to table.

"I've a sup of hot milk in the kitchen," remarked Katie, "an' I'll get it for her. I've heard it's lucky to feed a cat, an' when I go back to the old country,—an' I'm goin' soon now,—I hope a black cat will walk in for a visit, the very first day I'm home again." And with this, she took Pussy in through the window and went out into the kitchen.

"Sometimes I wonder how I should get along without Katie," said Mrs. Paulding, "and then, when she frightens you as she did just now, and overrides us all, I almost wish she *would* go back to Ireland."

"We should never get another like her," Pauline declared, "and she is so good to the pussies."

"I believe you think of them first," her mother said, smiling.

"The poor things can't speak for themselves, Mama," the little girl responded; "somebody must think for them."

The clock on the mantel struck eight.

"Tom will be late," said Mrs. Paulding.

"No, he won't," cried her son, as he hastily entered the room. He kissed his mother, and then he took his seat at the table.

CHAPTER V.

AT THE BREAKFAST-TABLE.

MRS. PAULDING watched Tom eat about half of his bowl of oatmeal. Then she asked gently, "How is it you were late, my son?"

"I overslept myself," Tom answered, "and when Polly knocked at the door I was having a wonderful dream.

"It was about everything all mixed up, just as it is generally in dreams," went on Tom, "but it began with my floating around the room. I often dream I can float about in the air just as naturally as walking on the floor; and, in my dream, when I float around, nobody seems at all surprised, any more than if it was the most ordinary thing to do.

"I dreamed that I floated out to Mount Vesuvius, where there was an eruption going on and the flames were pouring out of the crater. There I heard cries of distress, and I found seven great genies had tied a fairy to a white marble altar, and they were dancing about her, and making ready to stone her with sticky lumps of red-hot lava. So I floated over to her and asked her what I could do for her—"

"Did n't the seven evil spirits see you?" interrupted Polly.

"They did n't in the dream," Tom answered, "though now I don't understand why they did n't."

"Perhaps the fairy had made you invisible," explained his sister.

"That may have been the way," Tom admitted. "So I floated over to the altar and I asked what I could do for her, and she whispered to stoop down and try if I could see three flat stones in the ground—"

"Did you see them?" interrupted Polly again.

"I did," said Tom; "and if you 'll just let me go on, you 'll get to the end of this story a sight sooner."

"I won't say another word," Pauline said.

"The three flat stones were just under my feet," said Tom. "The fairy told me to lift the center stone and she said that I should find under it a large copper ring—"

"And did y——" began Polly. "Oh!" and she suddenly stopped.

"She told me to pull on the ring and I would find an iron box," Tom went on, "and in that box was a beautiful silver-mounted, seven-shot revolver loaded with seven magic bullets with which I was to kill the seven genies. So I took the revolver and I shot the seven genies, one after the other; and then I released the fairy."

"What did she give you?" asked Polly, eagerly.

"If you don't say a word," Tom continued, "I will inform you that she gave me three wishes."

"What did you wish for?" Polly asked at once. "I know what I should like. I'd ask for a little bag containing all the things they have in fairy stories—a cap that makes you invisible, and shoes that make you go fast, and a carpet to carry you through the air, and all the things of that sort. You see it is always so awkward to have the wrong things; for instance, when there's a great, big, green dragon coming to eat you up and you want to be invisible all at once and in a hurry, it is n't any use having a purse that is always full of money. I should ask for them all—and if she was a real generous fairy, she'd count that as only one wish."

When his sister had finished this long speech, Tom was calmly eating the last of his oatmeal. She looked at him and cried:

"Tom, you are just too aggravoking for anything. What were your three wishes?"

"I don't know," answered Tom.

"Why not?" asked Pauline.

"Because," Tom responded, leisurely, "you interrupted me in my dream exactly as you did just now. That was as far as I'd got when you waked me up."

"Oh, oh!" said Polly. "If I'd known you were going to have three wishes, I would n't have called you for anything in the world. What *were* you going to wish for?" she went on. "Don't you remember now?"

"I don't know what I should have wished for in the dream,"

Tom answered; "but I know what I should wish for now, if a real, live, sure-enough fairy gave me one wish. I'd wish that mother's income were just twice as big as it is, so that she should n't have to worry about the mortgage and our clothes and my education."

Mrs. Paulding held out her hand, and Tom gave it a squeeze.

"You would be glad to have that Purse of Fortunatus that Pauline despised so," she said. "And so should I. The mortgage does bother me, now and then,—and there are other things, too. I wish I had enough to let you study engineering, since your mind is made up that you would like that best."

"My mind is made up that I'd like best to be an engineer, if I could," Tom responded; "but I sha'n't complain a bit if I have to go into a store next year."

"I hope that I shall at least be able to keep you at school," said his mother.

"I'd like to study for a profession, mother, as you know," he went on; "but I'm not willing to have you worry about it."

"I think I'd like to study for a profession, too," interrupted Pauline. "I'd like to learn doctory. We begin physiology next term, and they have a real skeleton for that —ugh! it will be great fun."

"You need not shiver in anticipation," said her mother, with a laugh.

"Tom," Polly asked, seriously, "did you ever have convulsions? You know I did—and when I was only two years old, too. So when we girls get a-talking over the things we've all had, measles and mumps, and they find out I have n't had whooping-cough,—why, then I just tell them I've had convulsions; and they have n't, not one of them."

"Mother," said Tom, who had been thinking quietly while his sister rattled on, "you told me once about some money that my great-grandfather lost. Did n't anybody ever try to find it?"

"Yes," Mrs. Paulding answered. "Your grandfather made a great search for it, so your father told me; and at one time he thought he was very 'warm,' as children say, but he suddenly seemed to lose all interest in it, and gave over the hunt all at once."

"Why?" asked Tom, eagerly.

"I don't know why," answered Mrs. Paulding; "nor did your father know, either."

"How did my great-grandfather lose the money?" Tom continued.

"It was stolen from him," replied his mother. "He was a paymaster in Washington's army; and when the British captured New York, the American army retreated up the island and held the upper part. A large sum of money had been paid to your great-grandfather—or rather he had raised it on his own property, for I believe that the stolen gold was his own and not the government's."

"And when was it stolen?" asked Tom.

"I think I heard your father say that it was taken from his grandfather during the night—during the night before the battle of Harlem Plains."

"That was in 1776," said Tom, "in September. Our teacher told us all about it only two or three weeks ago. And it was fought just around the corner from here, between Morningside Park and Central Park. Was Nicholas Paulding robbed during the fight?"

"Really, my son," responded Mrs. Paulding, "I know very little about it. Your father rarely spoke of it; it seemed to be a sore subject with him. But I think the robbery took place late that evening, after the battle was over,—or it may have been the night before."

"Who was the robber?" asked Tom. "They know who he was, don't they?"

"Yes," said his mother, "I think it is known who took the money. He was a deserter from our army. His name was Kerr, or Carr. He disappeared and the money was missing at the same time."

"Did n't you say once that the thief was never heard of after the stealing?" said Tom.

"That is what I have always understood," his mother declared. "The man left our army and was never seen again. After the war your grandfather made a careful search for him, but he could find no trace."

"Did n't the British receive him when he ran away? I thought the armies in that war were always glad to receive deserters from the other side."

"I think he never reached the British at all."

"Then what did become of him?" asked Tom.

"That is the mystery," replied his mother. "It was a mystery to your great-grandfather at the time and when the war was over; and it seems to have puzzled and interested your grandfather, too, at least for a while."

"It interests me," Tom declared. "I like puzzles. I wish I knew more about this one."

"There are a lot of papers of your grandfather's, maps and letters and scraps of old newspapers, somewhere in an old box where your grandfather put them more than fifty years ago," said Mrs. Paulding.

"And where is that box now?" was Tom's eager question.

"I think that it is in one of the old trunks in the attic," Mrs. Paulding replied.

Before Tom could say anything more, a shrill whistle was heard.

"There's the postman!" cried Pauline, jumping up from the breakfast-table. "I hope he has brought a letter for me!"

The Careful Katie entered and gave Mrs. Paulding a letter, saying, "It's a new letter-man, this one, and he says he ought to have left this letter yesterday. More fool he, say I."

With that she took the coffee-pot from the table and went out of the room again.

Mrs. Paulding looked at the handwriting for a moment and said, "It is from Mr. Duncan." Then she opened it and glanced at the signature and exclaimed, "Yes, it is from Mr. Duncan. I wonder what he has to say."

Tom knew that Mr. Duncan was a lawyer, and an old friend of the family, and that he had always advised Mrs. Paulding in business affairs. As his mother read, Tom watched her face. When she had finished the letter she let it fall in her lap.

"Well, mother," he asked, "have you received bad news?"

"Yes," she answered, "bad news indeed. Mr. Duncan writes that the gentleman who holds the mortgage on the house wishes us to pay it off soon, and Mr. Duncan is afraid that we shall not be able to get as much from anybody else."

"Well, suppose we don't?" Tom inquired.

"Then we shall have to sell this house and move away," said Mrs. Paulding; and she sank back in the chair, and with difficulty kept back her tears.

Pauline, who had been a silent spectator, walked over and put her arms about her mother. "How soon shall we have to go?" she asked.

"I hope we shall not have to go at all," Mrs. Paulding answered. "Mr. Duncan says that we have several months before us to see what we can do. Perhaps the mortgagee won't want his money before that time."

"Or perhaps Uncle Dick will come back with lots and lots of money," suggested Pauline.

"Mother," said Tom, suddenly, while he strapped up his school-books, "would you let me look at that box of papers —about that stolen gold?"

"Certainly, my son, if you would like to see them," she answered.

"How much money was it that my great-grandfather lost?" he asked.

"I don't know exactly. I think I once told you as much as the thief could carry comfortably—about two thousand pounds, perhaps."

"Whew! That's ten thousand dollars!" exclaimed Tom, as he bade her good-by before going to school. "Don't worry about that mortgage. I'm going to see if we can't get back some of that stolen money. Nobody knows where it is, and I may be lucky enough to find out. At any rate, I mean to try."

"'I'M GOING TO SEE IF WE CAN'T GET BACK SOME OF THAT STOLEN MONEY,' SAID TOM."

CHAPTER VI.

THE BOX OF PAPERS.

OWEVER much men may differ in the five quarters of the globe, boys are alike the world over. Wherever they may be born, and whatever be their bringing up, the quality of boyishness is sure to be in all of them. When the little cockney lad in the dark lanes of London hears the sound of Bow Bells, he cannot help sometimes putting himself in the place of Whittington, and, by sheer force of make-believe, succeeds in owning a cat, and in disposing of it for a high price to the Barbary king. No doubt the little Arab of Bagdad plays at Haroun al Raschid, and makes up out of his own head a tale of which he is the hero — one that in unexpectedness of adventure and in variety of incident far surpasses any told by the fair Scheherazade to the cruel Sultan in the watches of the "Thousand and One Nights."

So it is no wonder that the boys of America delight in being Indians. The condition of the streets and parks near the house where Tom Paulding lived was very well adapted for redskin raids, sudden ambushes, and long scouts after a retreating tribe of hostiles. Rarely a week passed that the Black Band did not go upon the war-path. And it was therefore with no surprise that Tom was called upon by Cissy Smith and Corkscrew Lott, the next Saturday morning, and was by them bidden to hurry over to Morningside Park as soon after dinner as he could.

Tom was kept busy at school during all the week; and Saturday was the only day when he really had any time to himself. In the morning he had usually a few errands to run for his mother and a few chores to do about the house. The afternoon was always his own.

"What are you going to do to-day?" asked Tom.

"We've got a mighty good idea," Cissy replied. "We are going over to Morningside to play the 'Death of Custer in the Lava Beds.'"

"That is a good scheme," Tom said. "Whose was it?"

"Harry Zachary suggested it," answered Smith. "He said that, if we did, we could have a bully massacree, and that we could pretend to kill them all off one by one."

"Harry has first-rate notions about a good fight," Tom declared. "I'd like to join in, but I can't."

"Why not?" asked Corkscrew.

"Well," said Tom, with a sense of the importance of the disclosure he was about to make, "I have some business to attend to. You remember that stolen gold I said belonged to us if we could only find it?"

"Yes," Cissy replied.

"Have you found out where it is?" asked Lott, eagerly.

"No," Tom answered; "at least not yet. But my mother has given me all the papers—a whole box full of them—and I'm going over them this afternoon."

"Shucks!" said Cissy, scornfully. "If you don't know where the gold is, what's the use of looking for it?"

"I hope to find a clue—that's what the detectives call it, is n't it?" Tom responded.

"All the clues you find," returned Cissy, "you can clue yourself up with! You had better come over to Morningside, instead of staying at home looking at old papers."

"What sort of papers are they?" inquired Lott. "Newspapers?"

"All sorts," Tom replied; "newspapers and old letters and reports; lots and lots of them. I have n't sorted them out yet, but they seem to be very interesting."

"Would you like me to come around and help you?" asked Lott.

"No," responded Tom, "I am going to find that gold myself, if it's to be found at all."

"I don't believe it's to be found at all," said Cissy. "I don't believe there ever *was* any to be found anywhere. This is just a sort of ghost-story they are fooling you with. I'll tell you what you had better do. You come over with us this afternoon, and we'll let you be Custer."

This was a temptation to Tom, and for a moment he wavered.

"We'd let you be the Indian Chief, Rain-in-the-Face,"

Cissy went on, noticing Tom's hesitation, "but Harry said, as he 'd suggested it, he thought he ought to be the Indian chief and lead in the scalping. But you can be Custer, if you 'll come."

"I 'd like to," answered Tom, who had made up his mind now, "but I can't. I 'm going over these papers this afternoon."

"If you find out anything, will you tell me?" Lott inquired.

"I 'll see," was Tom's response.

"He 'll tell you all he finds out," declared Cissy, as he rolled away, "and so could I—for he won't find out anything. As I said before, I don't believe there 's anything to find out."

This discouraging remark was intended for Tom's ear, and it had its due effect. Tom had a great respect for Cissy Smith's judgment. For a few seconds he wondered whether it was really worth while to give up a beautiful day just to turn over a lot of dusty old papers in the wild hope of finding something which the owner of the papers had ceased to seek long before he died.

But he had made his choice and he stuck to it. After the midday dinner of the family, Tom's resolve was fixed as if it had never faltered. His mother had given him permission to take the box of papers from a trunk in the attic where it had been ever since the death of Nicholas Paulding; and early in the morning he had gone up and opened the trunk and lifted out the box. As soon as he had finished his dinner, he went upstairs to his own room and locked his door. Then he emptied out upon his bed all the papers in the box.

THE BOX OF PAPERS.

The tumbled heap was about a foot high, and it contained one hundred and twenty-seven separate pieces. There were letters of his great-grandfather's. There were letters from and to his grandfather. There were copies of official documents. There were newspapers, and there were single articles cut from newspapers. There were old maps, marked over with notes in Wyllys Paulding's handwriting. There was a pamphlet printed in London in 1776, and giving a full and detailed account of the taking of New York by His Majesty's Forces. There were several old magazines with descriptions of the events which preceded and followed the battle of Harlem Heights. This pamphlet and these magazines contained notes in red ink by the hand of Wyllys Paulding. Most important of all was a statement, addressed in the handwriting of Tom's great-grandfather, in which Nicholas told his son the whole story of the stolen guineas.

Tom wondered why it was that his grandfather, having taken so much interest in the search for the stolen gold, should have abandoned it suddenly. This wonder, strong in the beginning, kept coming back again and again as Tom pursued his quest; and it grew stronger with every return. A day was to come when Tom would understand why his grandfather had so suddenly given up the search. For the time, and for a long while afterward, Tom could see no reason for this strange action.

With the aid of the statement Nicholas Paulding had written for Wyllys Paulding, the grandson of the latter was able to learn the exact circumstances under which the money had disappeared. Tom had to puzzle out and piece together, but at last he got at all the facts so far as it was possible to discover them.

Here, then, is an orderly account of events from the time the treasure came into the possession of Nicholas Paulding to the hour of its disappearance and the disappearance of the man who had stolen it:

When General Washington had his headquarters in New York, after the battle of Long Island, Nicholas Paulding mortgaged his houses and lots near the Battery for the large sum of two thousand guineas. He had great difficulty in getting any one to lend him the money. In those troublous times, when none knew what might be the future of the colonies, few men were willing to part with the gold in their possession. At last, however, Nicholas Paulding found a man willing to let him have the money on his bond and mortgage. This man was a newly arrived German, and his name was Horwitz—Simon Horwitz. He was very particular about the form of the papers; and even after all the papers had been drawn up to his complete satisfaction, he delayed the payment of the money. It was not until Saturday, September 14, 1776, when the Continental army was leaving New York, and when the patriots were flocking out of the city, knowing that the British might take possession at any hour—it was not until then that Simon Horwitz finally accepted the bond and mortgage of Nicholas Paulding and paid over the two thousand guineas.

Nicholas Paulding was a very young man, barely of age.

"TOM HAD TO PUZZLE OUT AND PIECE TOGETHER, BUT AT LAST HE GOT AT ALL THE FACTS SO FAR AS IT WAS POSSIBLE TO DISCOVER THEM."

He had been at King's College (as Columbia College was then called) with Alexander Hamilton, and he was scarcely second to that great man in devotion to the cause of his country. He had early enrolled himself in Washington's army, and he had been chosen to act as paymaster of a New York regiment. The post was honorable but laborious, for the soldiers would expect their pay regularly and there was little money in the treasury. It was as his contribution to the cost of the struggle for liberty that Nicholas Paulding had borrowed two thousand guineas on the security of his homestead. He intended to devote the money to the payment of the men in his regiment as there might be need.

As soon as he had counted the coins received from Simon Horwitz, Nicholas Paulding tied them up in four canvas bags, sealing the knots with wax, on which he impressed his seal. Then he concealed these bags about his person as best he could. He was a stalwart man, of full stature and unusual strength for his years, but the weight of these bags must have been an inconvenient burden. Two thousand guineas would be worth more than ten thousand dollars; they would be in bulk a little more than a thousand solid eagles; and they would weigh not far from forty pounds.

Early on the morning of Sunday, September 15, the day after Nicholas Paulding had received his money, three British men-of-war sailed boldly by the Battery and entered the Hudson River. Every one knew then that the city was doomed to fall into the hands of the King's forces in a few hours. The American troops made ready to retreat, and there were none to oppose the landing of the British soldiers as they crossed from Long Island under cover of the fire of the fleet. Nicholas Paulding was with some men who made a stand against a regiment of Hessians in the fields across which ran the Boston Road (near what is now the corner of Third Avenue and Twenty-third Street). Then the Americans fell back and joined the main body of the Continental army retiring on Harlem Heights. The rain poured in torrents, and there sprang up a chill wind. The men of Paulding's regiment were footsore from their long march when they halted for the night a little above Bloomingdale, and not far from the eight-mile stone.

They found small comfort in their hasty camp, a smoky fire of damp wood, what food they had with them and no more,—no tents and no blankets. Upon the sodden earth they laid them down to sleep; and despite the raging of the storm, most of them were so tired that they slept soundly.

With his fellow-officers, Nicholas Paulding had done his share in seeing to the safety and the comfort of his men. After the sentries were placed, he joined his companions in consultation as to the work for the next day. Then he went to the place set apart for him, before a smoking fire beaten by the pelting rain; and there he lay down to sleep, if he could. A man named Jeffrey Kerr had been serving as paymaster's clerk, and to this fellow Nicholas Paulding had confided the fact that he had two thousand guineas concealed about his person. This Kerr was lying before the camp-fire, apparently asleep, when Nicholas Paulding settled himself for the night; the clerk was wrapped in a huge, loose surtout with enormous pockets.

How long Nicholas Paulding slept he did not know, but he remembered a faint dream of a capture by brigands who felt about his body and robbed him of his treasure. When he slowly awakened, he was being turned from his side over to his back, and some one was loosening the belt which sustained the bags of guineas. The night was blacker than ever, and the rain was pouring down in sheets. Still almost asleep, he resisted drowsily and gripped the belt with his hands. When the belt was pulled from his grasp, he awoke and sprang to his feet. In the black darkness before him he could see nothing; but his hand, extended at a venture, clasped a rough coat.

Then there came a dazzling flash of lightning, and Nicholas Paulding found himself face to face with the man Kerr, who had hold of the belt and the four pendent bags of treasure. The two men were almost in the center of the storm; the lightning had struck a tree between them and the British troops; but before the clap of thunder followed the flash, Jeffrey Kerr smote the man he was trying to rob and forced him to let go the coat. Whether Kerr had seized a limb of a tree lying there ready for the fire, or whether he had used as a weapon the belt itself with the treasure-bags attached, the robbed man never knew.

Nicholas Paulding was stunned for a moment, but he soon recovered and gave the alarm. As the thief passed the sentry he was fired at, but in the dense darkness the shot went wide of its mark, and Kerr rushed on through the lines of the American army.

He was familiar with the region. He had been a clerk with Colonel Morris at the Red Mill, and knew every foot of that part of Manhattan Island. It was well for him that he did, else he never could have escaped from his pursuers, in spite of the blackness of the night. He was within thirty yards of a second sentry when another flash of lightning revealed him again.

The soldier fired at once. There was a slight cry of pain; but the man could not have been wounded severely, since Nicholas Paulding, with a company of the men of his regiment, carefully examined the ground where Kerr had stood at the moment of firing, and thence down a hundred yards or so, to a little brook, which divided the lines of the Americans from the British, and across which it was not safe to venture, even if the rain-storm had not so swollen the stream as to make a crossing dangerous in the darkness.

And after that hour Nicholas Paulding had no news of his treasure, and no man ever laid eyes on Jeffrey Kerr.

The morning following the robbery, there was fought the Battle of Harlem Heights, which was a decided victory for the Continental army.

Encouraged greatly by the result of this fight, the American forces lay intrenched on Harlem Heights for three weeks, facing the British troops, separated from them by barely three hundred yards, the width of the little valley of Manhattanville. During these three weeks, Nicholas Paulding made every possible search for the man who had robbed him, but without learning anything. From prisoners taken during the Battle of Harlem Heights he inquired whether any deserter had been received in the British lines on the night of September 15, but he could hear of none.

A month later most of Washington's army was marched away from Manhattan Island, to do its part in the long and bloody struggle of the Revolution.

For seven years Nicholas Paulding did not set foot in the city of New York, which was held for George III. until the close of the war.

When the cause of the patriots had triumphed, and the British troops had departed, Nicholas Paulding seems to have made but few inquiries after his stolen guineas. Apparently, in the wanderings and hardships of the Continental army, he had made up his mind that the money was gone and that any further effort was useless. Besides, he did not feel any pressing need of it, as he made money after the war was over, being able to buy lands and to build the house where his descendants were to live during the most of the next century.

But early in this century, when Wyllys, Nicholas Paulding's only son and Tom's grandfather, was nearing manhood, the tide of fortune turned and several successive investments were most unfortunate. Long before the War of 1812 the lost two thousand guineas would have been very welcome again. Even then Nicholas Paulding seemed to take little interest in the quest—at least all the correspondence was carried on by Wyllys. The statement of the circumstances of the robbery written by Nicholas bore an indorsement that it was drawn up "at the Special Request of my Son, Wyllys Paulding, Esq."

The first thing Wyllys Paulding tried to do was to hunt down Jeffrey Kerr; but he had no better luck than his father. Tom found among the papers two letters which showed how carefully Wyllys had conducted the search. One was from the British officer who had commanded the King's troops encamped opposite the regiment in which Nicholas Paulding served on the night of Sunday, September 15, 1776. This letter was dated London, October 10, 1810; and in it the British officer declared that he remembered distinctly the night before the Battle of Harlem Heights, and that he was certain that if a deserter had entered their lines that night he would surely recall it; but he had no such recollection; and on looking in the journal which he had kept all through the war, from his landing in New York to the surrender at Saratoga, he found no account there of any deserter having come in on the night in question; and he felt certain, therefore, that Kerr had not been received by his Majesty's forces. This letter was indorsed, in Wyllys's handwriting:

"A Courteous Epistle: the Writer, having survived the seven years of the Revolution and the Continental Wars of Buonaparte, was killed at the Battle of New Orleans."

The second of these letters was from a clergyman at New London, evidently a very old man, judging by the shaky handwriting. It was dated February 22, 1811. The writer declared that he had known Jeffrey Kerr as a boy in New London, where he was born, and that even as a boy Kerr was not trusted. His fellow-townsmen had been greatly surprised when they heard in 1776 that he was appointed paymaster's clerk, and they had remarked then that it was just the position he would have chosen for himself. The news of his robbery of his superior and of his flight had caused no wonder; it was exactly what was expected. Kerr had not been seen by any of his townsmen since he had left New London to join the army, and nothing had ever been heard of him. There was a general belief that he was dead; and this ripened into certainty when the wife he had left behind him inherited a fortune and he never came back to share it with her. The wife was firmly convinced that she was a widow; and so, in 1787, she had married again.

Upon this letter Wyllys Paulding had indorsed, "Can the man have been shot the night he stole the money? We know he did not reach the British lines, and now we are told that he never returned home, though he had every reason to do so. Well, if he be dead, where is our money?"

Among the other papers were cuttings from *Rivington's New York Gazetteer or the Connecticut, New Jersey, Hudson's River and Quebec Weekly Advertiser;* a folded sheet of paper on which was written "Notes of Horwitz's confession, Dec. 13, 1811," but which was blank on the other side (nor could Tom find any writing that might seem to belong within the cover of this paper); a letter from a fellow-officer of Nicholas Paulding's who was with him on the night of the robbery and who set forth the circumstances very much as Nicholas himself had already recorded them; and, most important of all, a rough outline map of the positions of the American and British troops on the night of September 15, 1776. This map had been sketched from memory by Nicholas Paulding, whose name it bore, with the date January, 1810.

On this map Nicholas had marked in red ink his own position when he was robbed, and the positions of the two sentries who had fired at Jeffrey as the thief fled in the darkness.

There were many other papers in the box besides those here mentioned, but the most of them did not seem to have anything to do with the stolen money.

There were not a few letters in answer to inquiries about Jeffrey Kerr; there were many newspapers and cuttings from newspapers; and there were all sorts of odds and ends, memoranda, and stray notes—such, for instance, as a calculation of the exact weight of two thousand guineas.

Tom went through them all, laying aside those which seemed to contain anything of importance. When he had examined every paper in the heap on his bed, he had two piles of documents before him: one was large and contained the less important papers and newspapers; the other was smaller, as it held only those of real importance.

Tom took the papers in the smaller heap and set out to arrange them in order by their dates.

When this was done he made a curious discovery. They were all the work of little more than two years.

Wyllys Paulding seemed to have started out to search late in 1809—and there was no document of any kind bearing date in 1812. Although he had not found what he was seeking and what he had sought most diligently at least for two years, it seemed as if he had suddenly tired and desisted from his quest.

So it was when Tom Paulding went to bed that night he had three questions to which he could find no answers:

I. What became of Jeffrey Kerr?

II. If Kerr was killed, what became of the two thousand guineas?

III. Why did Wyllys Paulding suddenly abandon all effort to find the stolen money?

CHAPTER VII.

CAKES AND A COMPOSITION.

EVERAL successive Saturday afternoons Tom Paulding devoted to the box of old papers, carefully going over every letter twice or thrice, that he might make sure of its full meaning and of its exact bearing on the problems to be solved. With like industry he read through the old newspapers and the cuttings therefrom which made up more than half the contents of the box. In these newspapers Tom found nothing relating to his investigation; but he discovered much in them that was amusing; and the glimpse of old New York they gave seemed to him so strange that Tom began to take interest in the early history of his native city. The more thoroughly he came to know the annals of New York, the prouder he was that he and his had been New-Yorkers for five generations at least.

One Saturday morning, early in December, about a month after Mrs. Paulding had given her son permission to take the box of old papers, Tom was going out to get his mother the ingredients for a batch of cakes she had to bake for a

CAKES AND A COMPOSITION.

customer. Mrs. Paulding was fond of cooking, and she made delicious broths and jellies; but her special gift was for baking cake. When the New York Exchange for Woman's Work was opened, Mrs. Paulding sent to it for sale a Washington pie, made after a receipt which had been a tradition in the family, even before the days of Mrs. Nicholas Paulding, Tom's great-grandmother. The purchaser of this delicacy was so delighted with it that she went again to the exchange and asked for another. So in time it came about that Mrs. Paulding was one of the ladies who eke out a slender income by making soups, jellies, and cakes to order for the customers of this Woman's Exchange.

In this pleasant labor Tom and Pauline were always anxious to aid. Polly had much of her mother's lightness of touch, and was already well skilled as a maker of what she chose to call "seedaway cake,"—because it was thus that she first had tried to name a cake flavored with caraway seeds. Tom had no liking for the kitchen, but he was glad to do what chores he could and to run all his mother's errands. Besides, Mrs. Paulding, with motherly forethought, was wont to contrive that there should be left over, now and again, small balls of dough, which she molded in little tins and baked for Tom and for Polly. These, however, were accidental delights to which they looked forward whenever their mother had a lot of cakes to make.

The Careful Katie did not always approve of Mrs. Paulding's invasion of her kitchen to make cake for others; but she always was pleased to see the little cakes which might lie a-baking in a corner of the oven as a treat for Tom and for Polly.

"It's a sweet tooth they have, both o' the childer," she said.

Polly had just called to her brother, "Oh, Tom, don't go out till you have given me that 'rithmetic of yours!"

"All right," answered her brother.

Just then Katie left the room, and Polly again delayed Tom's departure.

"When you were little," she said, "and Katie used to say you had a sweet tooth in your head, did it make you open your mouth, and feel your teeth, and wonder why she said you had only one? Because I did,—and I used to be afraid that perhaps if I ate too much cake I might lose my sweet tooth and not be able to taste it any more."

"You did lose all that set of sweet teeth, my dear," remarked Mrs. Paulding, smiling at Polly, as she weighed out the powdered sugar for her frosting.

"But I've got a new set of them," Polly replied, "and I'm sure that I like cake now more than ever."

"There was one of Katie's sayings that used to worry me," said Tom; "and that was when she pretended to be tired of talking to us, and declared that she would n't waste her breath on us. That made me think that perhaps we had only just so much breath each, and that if we wasted it when we were young, we should n't have any left when we were grown up—"

"I used to think that too," interrupted Pauline.

"And I thought that it would be horrible," continued her

brother, "to be an old man, and not be able to speak. So when I went to bed, sometimes I used to save my breath, keeping it in as long as I could."

"I wish I'd thought of that," Polly declared. "But I did n't. Now, where's that 'rithmetic?" she added, seeing that her brother had again started to go.

"I'll get it for you," Tom answered. "It's in my room."

In a minute he returned with the book in his hand.

Across the cover were written the following characters:

$$\tau o\mu \ \pi a \upsilon \lambda \delta \iota \nu \gamma \text{'}\varsigma \ \beta o o \chi.$$

Polly took the volume, and, seeing this strange legend, she asked at once, "What's that?"

"That?" echoed Tom. "Oh, that's Greek."

Mrs. Paulding looked around in surprise.

"I did not know you were studying Greek," she said.

"I'm not," Tom answered. "That is n't really Greek. It's just my name in Greek letters—I got them out of the end of the dictionary, you know. Besides, I did that years ago. I have n't used that book since I was eleven."

Then he took the list of things his mother wished him to get, and went out.

When he came back, Pauline danced out to meet him, waving a paper above her head with one hand, while with the other she kept tight hold of the kitten which had climbed to her shoulder.

"Guess what I've found!" she cried; "and guess where I found it!"

Tom went into the dining-room to make his report to his mother. Then he turned to Polly and said: "Well, and what did you find?"

"I found this—in your 'rithmetic," she answered, opening the paper and holding it before him. "It's one of your compositions, written when you were younger than I am now—when you were only ten. It's about money—and Marmee and I don't think that it is so bad, considering how very young you were when you wrote it."

Mrs. Paulding smiled, but said nothing.

"'GUESS WHAT I'VE FOUND!' SHE CRIED."

"Let me see!" cried Tom, holding out his hand.

"Will you promise to give it back?" she asked, retreating behind her mother.

"It's mine, is n't it?" he replied.

"But I want to keep it. I would like to show it to our teacher and to some of the girls, because it is so funny. I can tell them that a little boy wrote it, without telling who it was. It was a good subject to write about, I think. Just think what I've got to do a composition on next week! On 'Loyalty!' What can I write about Loyalty? That's one of those head-in-the-air words I never have anything to say about. The teachers we had last year used to let us write descriptive compositions. I wrote one on 'A Walk in Riverside Park,' and I told all about the little girl's tomb with the urn on it, you know. And we kept changing teachers, and I handed in that composition three times!"

"O Pauline!" said her mother, reproachfully.

"Well," the little girl explained, "I wrote it over every time and made it longer and fixed it up a bit. It's so hard to think of things to say when you have to write a composition."

"Let me have mine now," said Tom, "and I'll give it back."

"Honest?" she asked.

"Certain sure," he answered.

"Hands across your heart?" she inquired, holding out the paper.

"Never see the back of my neck again, if I don't!" declared Tom, taking it from her hand hastily.

When he had opened it, and when he saw the irregular handwriting and the defective spelling, he blushed slightly.

"I wrote this when I was a boy," he said, apologetically.

"What are you now?" asked his mother, as she glanced up from her labors, smiling.

"I mean a little boy," Tom answered.

This is the composition which Tom Paulding had written

when he was "a little boy." The signature and the date under it are omitted, but the latter showed that Tom was just ten years and three months old when he composed it:

MONEY.

I   Money is one of the most useful things in the world
II   and if it was not for money we should not have
III half the comforts and emploments which we have. Money
IV   is a great thing and goes a great sometimes. There
V   are a great many kinds of coins of different nations
VI   the English, the French, the American, the Austriun, and the
VII Russian, and a great many others kinds of coins,
VIII There has been a great deal of money spent in
IX   the war, To pay the soldier, and to buy the imple-
X   ments of war, such as cannons, mortars, and cannans balls
XI   and powder, and some of it to give to the widows
XII of the soldierds who have been killed, There are
XIII two kinds of Money, one kind of which is paper
XIV and the other kind is speice which is coin such
XV   as gold silver and copper The coin, of the United
XVI, States are eagles, dollars, dimes, cents, and
XVII, mills, These are gold silver and copper. The
XVIII, Eagles dollars are gold, dollars dimes half dimes are sil-
XIX, ver, cents and half cents are copper., Besides the paper
XX   money of the United States, which are the 100, 10, 5
XXI dollars and less.

"What I like about it," said Polly, stooping so that the kitten could jump off her shoulder, "is the way you have numbered the lines. Those Xs and Vs take up a lot more space than plain figures, and they help to fill up beautifully Our teacher now wants us to write forty lines, but she won't let us number them—is n't that mean?"

"I suppose you could write a very different composition

on the same subject now, Tom, since you have been in search of the money stolen from your great-grandfather," Mrs. Paulding suggested.

"I don't know," Tom answered, with a laugh; "I think I have learned something about the history of the battles here in September, 1776; but I don't know any more about money, because I have n't found any yet."

"How do you get on with your search?" asked his mother.

"I don't get on at all," Tom answered, frankly. "I seem to have found out all there is to know — and that does n't tell me anything really. I know all about the stealing, but I have n't the first idea where the stolen money is."

"Then I would not waste any more time on it," said Mrs. Paulding.

"Oh, I 'm not going to give it up now," Tom declared, forcibly; "it 's just like a puzzle to me, and I 've worked over puzzles before. Sometimes you go a long while, and you don't see in the least how it could be done; and then, all of a sudden, it comes to you, and you do it as easily as can be. And that 's what I hope will happen about this two-thousand-guinea puzzle. At any rate, that 's the biggest prize I ever had a chance at, and I 'm not going to give it up without trying hard for it."

Mrs. Paulding's eyes lighted up with pleasure at Tom's energy.

"I wish your Uncle Dick were here to help you," she said.

"I 'd rather do it all by myself, if I can," Tom returned. "If I can't, then I 'd like Uncle Dick's help."

"Where is Uncle Dick now?" asked Pauline.

"I believe he is at the diamond-fields in South Africa," her mother answered. "That is where I wrote him last; but I have n't heard from him for nearly a year now."

"But if Uncle Dick came back, mother, we should n't need the two thousand guineas," said Tom; "he 'd pay off the mortgage, and send me to study engineering, and get a new doll for Polly, and—"

"I 'm not a baby!" interrupted Pauline, "and I don't want a new doll. If I had lots and lots of money, I think I should like a little teeny-weeny tiger—just a tiger-kitten, you know. It would be such fun to play with it. Is Uncle Dick very rich, Marmee?"

"I do not know whether he has any money at all or not," answered Mrs. Paulding. "He was always a rolling stone, and I doubt if he has gathered any moss."

"I should n't like an uncle who had about him anything so green as moss," said Tom.

"We 'd like to see him, if he had n't a cent," cried Polly. "But I 've read stories where uncles came back, and were ever so rich, and did everything you wanted, and paid off the mortgage, and gave everybody all the money they needed."

"I 'm afraid you must n't expect that kind of an uncle," sighed Mrs. Paulding.

"Then I wish we had a fairy godmother!" Polly declared.

"We 've got something finer than that," said Tom, bending forward and kissing Mrs. Paulding; "we 've got a mother better than any fairy."

CHAPTER VIII.

A QUARREL AND AN ARRIVAL.

IT must not be supposed that Tom Paulding's whole time was given up to his quest for the stolen guineas, or that he in any way neglected his studies at school or his duties at home. He went to school regularly, and he did his usual tasks much as he had done them before he had taken up the search; perhaps his interest in American history was a little keener now that he felt himself in touch with the soldiers of the Continental army. His liking for mathematics, and his ingenuity in solving problems, were no greater than before, as the science of numbers had always been his favorite branch of learning.

At home, as at school, life went on with the same round of duties and pleasures, the sameness of which was not relieved after Tom had set his mind on a single object. It was only on Saturdays, and then chiefly in the afternoon, that Tom could really devote himself to his quest. And this fixing of Tom's energies on a private enterprise caused a loosening of the tie that bound him to the Black Band. He lacked the time to take part in all the elaborate sports of his friends; and although, now and again, some specially wild plan of the delicate Harry Zachary might for a moment tempt him, he wavered for a moment only and went on his own way with little regret, leaving his friends to amuse themselves after their fashion.

At first this giving up of the pleasant sports of boyhood, even for a little while, was not easy; but as time went on, and as Tom became more and more deeply interested in the work to which he had given himself, he found that it was easier and easier to turn aside from the tempting suggestions of Harry Zachary and the hearty invitations of Cissy Smith. It seemed to Tom as if he had now a more serious object in life, to gain which would relieve not only himself, but his mother and his sister; and this thought strengthened him, and he ceased to regret in any way his lessened interest in the doings of the Black Band.

On the afternoon of the Saturday when Pauline had read his early composition on "Money," Tom took a map he had found in the boxes of papers. This was the map roughly outlined by Nicholas Paulding, and it showed the position of the American and British forces on the night of the robbery. On it were marked also the situation of the camp-fire where Nicholas had slept that evening, and the posts of the two sentries who had fired at the thief. It showed, moreover, the course of the little stream which separated the opposing armies. Tom intended to compare this map with the ground as it was now, and to see if he could identify any of the landmarks, and so make sure exactly where the robbery took place and in which direction Jeffrey Kerr had fled.

The weather was mild for the season of the year. It was almost the middle of December, and as yet there had been neither ice nor snow. A bright, clear December day in New York is, as Shakspere says of old age, "frosty, but kindly." Tom felt the bracing effect of the breeze as he stepped briskly along. What he wished chiefly to discover was a trace of the brook which the map indicated as having flowed between the camp of George Washington's men and the camp of the men of George III. He knew the ground fairly well already, but he did not recall any such stream.

As he was hurrying along he came suddenly upon a little group of the Black Band, marching down the street two abreast under command of Cissy Smith, who careened at the head.

"Hello, Tom!" cried Cissy Smith.

"Hello!" replied Tom.

"Halt!" commanded the leader of the Black Band. "Break ranks! Go as you please!"

Lott twisted himself forward and greeted Tom sneeringly:

"Hello, Curly! Are you off on your wild-goose chase now?"

"Look here, Corkscrew, I've told you before that I won't be called Curly! And you sha'n't do it any more," Tom declared, indignantly. He regretted bitterly that his dark hair persisted in curling, despite his utmost endeavor to straighten it out and to plaster it down.

"If I had hair like a girl's, all curls and ringlets, I should n't mind being called Curly," Corkscrew explained, a little sulkily.

"Well, I do mind," Tom said, emphatically; "and I want it stopped."

Lott was silent. Perhaps he had no answer ready. He was a little older than Tom, and of late he had begun to grow at a most surprising rate. He was already the tallest boy of the group. Cissy Smith had said that if Corkscrew only kept on growing, the Black Band would make him their standard-bearer and use him as the flagstaff, too. Lott's spare figure seemed taller and thinner than it was because of the high boots he always wore.

"I reckon there 'll be a row between Tom and Corkscrew, sooner or later," whispered Harry Zachary to Smith. "They are both of 'em just spoiling for a fight."

"Tom would knock the fight out of him in no time," Cissy answered. "He's well set up, while Lott's all out of shape, like a big clothes-pin. If he tried to bully me, I 'd tell him to stop it, or I 'd make him sorry."

Lott hesitated and then held out his hand to Tom. "I tell you what I 'll do," he said. "I 'll agree never to call you Curly again, if you 'll take me into this search of yours. I 'd like to know all about it, and I can find out a lot for you."

"Oh, ho!" cried Cissy. "I thought you called it a wild-goose chase?"

"So I did," Lott replied. "But that was only to tease Tom."

"I do not want any help," Tom declared.

"I'll do what I can," urged Lott. "And when we get it, I'll ask for only a third of the money."

"No," Tom replied. "I'm going to find it alone or not at all."

"I'll help you for a quarter of what we get—" Lott went on.

"There's no use talking about it," said Tom. "When I want a side-partner in this business, I'll pick one out for myself."

"All right," Corkscrew answered, with a sudden twist which took him out of the circle. "It's your loss, not mine. Any way, I don't believe you'll ever find anything, either."

At this juncture little Jimmy Wigger ran up breathlessly and joined the group of boys.

"Are you going to play any good games to-day?" he asked, eagerly. "Can't I play, too? I'd have been here before, but my aunt wouldn't let me till now. She's given me permission to be out two hours if I'm with Cissy or Tom, and if I promise to be very careful and not to get my feet wet."

"I'll take care of you," said Cissy.

"And we'll let you play with us, if you are a good boy, and don't cry," added Lott.

"I haven't cried for 'most a year now," little Jimmy declared, indignantly.

"Then see you don't cry to-day," said Lott, taking from

his pocket what was apparently a bit of wooden pencil. "Oh, I say, Jimmy, just hold this for me, will you, while I tie it?"

"Certainly," little Jimmy replied, willingly.

"Hold it this way," Lott explained, "between your thumb and your finger—so. Press tight against each end—that's it. Now I'll tie the string."

As Corkscrew took hold of the threads which came out of a hole in the middle of the pencil, and which, if pulled, would thrust two needles into little Jimmy's hand, Tom grabbed him by the arm.

"Drop that, Corkscrew!" he cried. "You sha'n't play that on Jimmy."

"Why not?" asked Lott. "I fooled you with it yesterday."

"I'm old enough to take care of myself," Tom answered. "Jimmy is n't. Besides, he's just been put under my care and Cissy's for to-day."

Lott sullenly wound the threads about the mean contrivance in preparing which he had spent his study hour the day before. As he put it in his pocket he said, "I don't see why some people can't mind their own business!"

"I'm going to make it my business to keep you from bullying Jimmy," Tom responded.

"How are you going to do it?" sneered Lott.

"I've been able to do it so far by catching you in time. But before we get through I believe we shall have to fight it out," Tom asserted.

"Oh, indeed!" Lott rejoined. "And who'll take you home to your mother then?"

"I'm younger than you," Tom answered, "and I'm not so big, but I don't believe you can hurt me. And I don't mean to have you hurt Jimmy here. Do you understand?"

"Oh, yes, I understand fast enough," Corkscrew rejoined; "and I shall do just what I like. So there!"

There was a little more talk among the boys, and then they parted. The Black Band marched off, Cissy Smith lurching ahead as captain, with little Jimmy Wigger and Corkscrew Lott in the ranks together. Tom went on his way to verify the map made by his great-grandfather.

"TOM WAS ABLE TO FIND MOST OF THE POSITIONS INDICATED ON THE MAP."

Just as the Black Band was going around a corner which would take them out of sight, Lott stopped and called back.

Tom turned in answer to this hail. What he heard was the taunting voice of Corkscrew shouting after him, "Good-by, Curly! Curly! Oh, Curly! Put them up in paper when you get home!"

Tom hesitated whether he should run after Lott and have their fight out once for all, or whether he should pay no attention to his words. He chose the latter course, and went on his way again.

During the afternoon, before the early twilight closed in, he was able to find most of the positions indicated on the map. Some of them were plainly to be seen, being very little changed from their condition the night before the Battle of Harlem Heights. Others were difficult to verify, because of the new streets and the houses which had been built of late years.

The little brook, which was the chief object Tom wished to trace, he succeeded at last in locating precisely. Of course it was no longer a brook. When streets are run across meadows and through hills, the watercourses must needs lie dry and bare. But there were several adjoining blocks where the street-level was higher than the original surface, and where the vacant lots had not been filled in.

Across three of these open spaces Tom was able to trace the course of the little stream, with its occasional rock-bordered pools, in which fish once used to feed, and which had become dry and deserted. The willows which bordered one bank of the brook were still standing. Tom was successful in discovering even the site of the Seven Stones which had served for a passage across the stream where it broadened out into a tiny pond.

In the plan made by Tom's great-grandfather these were marked "the stepping-stones" simply; but in another and rougher map, which also Tom had found among the papers of Wyllys Paulding, they were called the Seven Stones. Tom was interested in identifying them, as he thought that Jeffrey Kerr might have crossed them in his flight from the American camp to the British.

But as Kerr never reached the British forces, there was no need of speculating how it was that he might have gone if he had reached them. This Tom felt keenly. In fact the more he studied the situation, and the better he became acquainted with the surroundings, the more difficult seemed the problem of Kerr's disappearance. When that feeling was at its worst, he would recollect that his grandfather had made the same inquiries he was now trying to make, and that his grandfather had suddenly and unhesitatingly abandoned the quest; and the reason for this strange proceeding seemed to Tom as hard to seek as the other.

Tom walked slowly home in the gathering dusk of the December day. The sun was setting far down across the river, and the clouds were rosy and golden with the glow. Tom did not see the glories of nature; his mind was busy with his puzzles. He kept turning them over and over again. He wished that he had some one to whom he could talk plainly, and who might be able to suggest some new point of view. None of his school-fellows was available for this purpose. Corkscrew, of course, would not do, and Harry Zachary was too young, while Cissy Smith was so practical and so sarcastic sometimes that Tom hated to go to him, although he and Cissy were the best of friends.

His mother he was not willing to bother with his hopes and his fears. She had her own burdens. Besides, the delight of bringing her money to pay off the mortgage and do with as she pleased would be sadly damped if she had any share in the recovery of the guineas.

Tom found himself wishing that he had some older friend whom he could consult. He wondered even whether he might not do well to go down town and have a talk with the lawyer, Mr. Duncan.

When he had climbed the steep flight of wooden steps which led from the street to the ground about their house, he thought he saw Pauline at a window as though she were waiting for him. As he drew near the porch, the front door was opened and Pauline came flying out, her eyes sparkling and her hair streaming out behind.

"Tom," she cried; "oh, Tom, guess who is here!"

"I can't guess," he answered. "Who is it?"

"It's Uncle Dick," she answered. "He came this afternoon just after you went out, and I was all alone, and I had to receive him. And now he's in the parlor talking to Marmee and waiting to see you."

Here, as it happened, was the very friend Tom had been hoping for.

CHAPTER IX.

UNCLE DICK.

HEN Tom followed Pauline into the parlor he found his uncle seated on the sofa beside their mother. The first sight of his uncle gave Tom the impression of strength and heartiness, which was confirmed as they came to know each other well. Uncle Dick was neither tall nor stout, but his figure was well built and solid; perhaps he was rather under than over the average height of man. His eyes were dark, and so was his hair, save where it was touched with gray at the temples. His hands, which were resting on his knees, seemed a little large; and the distinct sinews of the wrists indicated unusual strength of grip. His face was clean shaven, except for the mustache which curled heavily down each cheek.

His smile was kindly as his eyes looked Tom straight in the face, and his greeting was hearty.

"So this is Tom, is it?" he said, holding out his hand and giving Tom a cordial clasp.

"And you are Uncle Dick," Tom responded, echoing his uncle's pleasant laugh.

"Yes, I am Uncle Dick. I'm your mother's only brother, and you are her only son. Let me get a good look at you."

So saying, he raised his hands and grasped Tom by the shoulders and held the boy off at arm's-length, while he took stock of him.

After a long searching gaze, which Tom met unflinchingly, Uncle Dick said to Mrs. Paulding, "He has your eyes, Mary, and your hair,— but how like he is to his father!"

Despite his bold front, Tom had endured the close scrutiny with secret discomfort; but now he flushed with pleasure. Mrs. Paulding had often talked to her son about the father he could scarcely remember, and it was Tom's chief wish to grow as like his father as he could.

"Yes," repeated Uncle Dick, "he is very like Stuyvesant." Then he released his hold on Tom's shoulders. "I do not see, Mary," he said, turning to Mrs. Paulding, "that you have any reason to be dissatisfied with these youngsters. They look like healthy young Americans with clear consciences and good appetites. If they take to me as I have taken to them, we shall get along all right."

"I'm sure we shall all be ever so fond of you, if you'll only stay here," said Pauline; "in fact, I'm fond of you now."

"You see, your sister and I," explained Uncle Dick to Tom, "have already made friends. She has shown me round her cat-ranch outside there, and —"

"And what do you think?" interrupted Pauline. "Mousie approved of Uncle Dick at once, and went up and let him

PAULINE AND UNCLE DICK INSPECTING THE "CAT-RANCH."

stroke his neck—and you know Mousie is very hard to please."

"Then I can look upon Mousie's approval of me as a certificate of good moral character," said Uncle Dick, with a ringing laugh. "And I don't know but what I'd rather have a letter of recommendation from a dumb beast than from many a man I've met. As a judge of human nature, 'the biped without feathers,' as Plato called him, is sometimes inferior to our four-footed friends."

"I'm glad to be told I'm like my father," Tom remarked, as he sat down by his mother's side.

"You are like him, as I've said," responded his uncle, "and that's a reason you and I should be good friends,—for no man ever had a better friend than your father was to me. When we were boys of your age we played together on these grounds; and we went off on long walks together up to High Bridge and across the Harlem River. This is a fine place for a boy—at least we found it so. There are lots of good spots for sham fights and so forth. Down in the woods by the river, near the railroad track, we used to go on long scouting-raids after the Indians. But I suppose that is altogether too old-fashioned a sport for you boys nowadays."

Tom promptly informed his uncle all about the Black Band, and about the bonfire on election night, when he had to run the gantlet and had afterward been burnt at the stake.

"Mother has told us about your adventure with the Indians in the Black Hills," Tom said; "that is, she's told us all you wrote, but there must be lots more to tell—is n't there?"

"There 's one thing to tell," replied Uncle Dick; "it 's a great deal more fun to play at Indians here on Manhattan Island than it is to have the real redskins come whooping after your scalp."

"They did n't get yours, did they?" asked Pauline.

"They did n't that time—but it was a very tight squeak," Uncle Dick answered.

"You 'll tell us about *all* your adventures, won't you?" Pauline besought.

Uncle Dick laughed heartily. "I 've been about a good deal, here and there, but I don't know that I 've really had any adventures that you could call adventures," he said.

"But you ran away to sea?" Polly cried.

"Oh, yes," he answered.

"And you were wrecked?" she continued.

"Yes," assented her uncle.

"And you went to the war, and you were taken prisoner?" she went on.

"Yes."

"And you 've fought the horrid Indians, and you 've been to Africa for diamonds, and you 've done lots and lots of other things like that,—and if those are not adventures, I 'd just like to know what are?" she urged.

"Some of these things were rather exciting while they lasted," said Uncle Dick, calmly, "but I don't think I should call any of them adventures."

"What would you call an adventure, then?" asked Pauline.

"Oh, I don't know," he replied. "Perhaps it is an adventure to have been shut up in the Rock Temple at Petra, alone with your deadly enemy, when he had a revolver and you had nothing but a penknife, and when you believed that if you got out alive the natives outside would promptly kill you."

"Did that happen to you?" asked Tom, with intense interest.

"Well, it was n't exactly that way," responded his uncle. "You see he had only a single-barreled pistol and I had a bowie-knife, so it was almost an even thing."

"Did you fight him?" Polly inquired.

"I had to."

"And how did it end?" Polly asked, eagerly. "Did he kill you?"

Uncle Dick laughed again and responded, "Do I look like a ghost?"

Polly blushed and explained hastily, "I mean, did you kill him?"

"No," her uncle said, "I did n't kill him and he did n't kill me. He fired at me and missed my head by half an inch — I believe he did cut off a stray lock of hair — you see I have curls like yours, Tom."

"And what did you do then?" was Polly's instant query.

"He sprang on me and I defended myself, and he got a wound—"

"A serious wound?" asked Polly.

"I never yet saw a wound that was comic," Uncle Dick replied, "either for the man who had it, or the man who gave it. Fighting is a sad business, at best, and I keep out of it when I can. As good luck would have it, this man's wound was not dangerous; but it left me free to make my escape."

"But how did you get past the natives outside, who were waiting to kill you?" asked Tom.

"I did n't get past them," was the answer.

"But they did n't *kill* you!" Polly cried.

"They got ready to do it," Uncle Dick explained, "when an old sheik interfered. He was a great friend of mine, that old sheik, and I had done him a favor once; and so he saved my life and got me away to the coast. Of course you ought to do people favors whenever you can; and the very least reason is that you never know when their gratitude may come in handy."

"How did you happen to be in the Rock Temple?" asked Tom, "and with your enemy, too?"

"How did I happen to get into all my scrapes?" returned Uncle Dick. "For a simple reason. Because I did not follow the advice of the Turkish proverb which says, 'Before you go in, find a way out.' All my life I 've been going into all sorts of things—and generally I 've had to squeeze out of the little end of the horn. As the old colonel of my regiment used to say, 'I 've had lots of luck in my life—good and bad.'"

"It is good luck which has brought you back to me, Dick," said Mrs. Paulding. "And the longer you stay the better I shall like it."

"I don't know how long it will be, Mary," he answered;

"that all depends on what Joshua Hoffmann says on Monday morning."

"Joshua Hoffmann?" Tom repeated; "is n't he the gentleman who owns that grand new house on the Riverside Drive, with the broad piazzas, and the towers, and the ground around it with a brick wall?"

"Yes," Mrs. Paulding replied. "Mr. Hoffmann has built a new house near us since you were here last, Dick."

"Everything around this place seems new since I was here last," Uncle Dick returned. "But even if Joshua Hoffmann has a house near us, I sha'n't intrude on him up here — at least not at first. I'll talk business down-town at his office."

"He's sure to be glad to see you, Dick," said Mrs. Paulding. "Children, you know that your uncle saved Mr. Hoffmann's life?"

"I did n't know it at all," Tom replied.

"Neither did I," Uncle Dick declared.

"Tell us all about it at once, please," Polly besought. "I like to hear about people's lives being saved."

"It's very little to tell," her uncle responded; "all I did was to give him warning of a plot against him. It was when he was out in the China Seas, aboard his private steam-yacht, the 'Rhadamanthus.' He had a crew of Lascars, and was going down the coast. From a Chinaman I had once recommended I received warning not to go — he'd offered me a berth on the yacht — because the Chinese pirates had bribed half the crew, and they meant to attack Mr. Hoffmann in a pirate junk which would come alongside under pretense of being in need of water. Of course I warned Mr. Hoffmann, and I accepted the berth on the yacht, and we made ready for a good fight. We ran out of port, dropped alongside an American man-of-war, sent back the treacherous crew, and took on board a lot of new men we could trust."

"And did the pirate junk attack you?" Tom asked, eagerly.

"It did," Uncle Dick answered. "And when they made their sudden assault and found us ready for them with a couple of Gatling guns on the main deck, you never saw pirates so surprised in all your life."

"I didn't know that Chinamen were ever pirates," said Polly; "I thought they all either made tea or took in washing."

"How did the fight end?" was Tom's impatient question.

"The junk was sunk, and the crew were sent back as prisoners; and I suppose that in time they were tried and sentenced."

At this juncture in the conversation, the Careful Katie entered to announce that supper was ready. Tom rushed upstairs to wash and to brush his hair.

When he came down, he found his mother and Uncle Dick discussing Mr. Joshua Hoffmann, who was at once one of the richest and one of the best men in New York; a man good himself and never tired of doing good to others; a man full of public spirit and leading in notable public enterprises; a man who considered his great fortune as a trust for the benefit of those who had been less fortunate.

"He's a man riches have not spoiled," remarked Uncle Dick; "and that's saying a great deal for anybody."

"He's a man that's good to the poor," interjected the Careful Katie. "Heaven bless him!"

For a second Uncle Dick looked a little surprised at this

UNCLE DICK TELLS TOM AND POLLY HIS ADVENTURES.

intrusion of the waitress into the conversation. Then he laughed softly to himself; and he said to his sister, as the Careful Katie left the dining-room to get the hot biscuits, "I see that she is quite as talkative as ever."

Mrs. Paulding smiled and answered, "She's a faithful creature, and I am used to her occasional loquacity."

"I like it," Uncle Dick responded; "I like anybody out of the common,—anybody or anything that has a character of its own. I have no use for a man who has had all his edges and corners smoothed off till he is just as round and as commonplace as his neighbors."

The Careful Katie returned and placed on the table a plateful of smoking hot biscuits. As she did this she dislodged a knife, which fell to the floor.

"That's a gentleman's coming to the house," she said, promptly. "Sure if I'd done it yesterday, I'd 'a' said it meant you comin' back to us to-day, Mr. Richard."

"So if you drop a knife it means a gentleman is coming to the house, does it?" asked Uncle Dick, with immediate interest. He had studied the folk-lore and strange beliefs of savage peoples in all parts of the world; and to find a superstition quite as absurd in the chief city of the United States, in the last quarter of the nineteenth century, was a surprise.

"What else should it mane?" answered Katie.

"And if you drop a fork," Uncle Dick continued, "I suppose that means a lady is coming?"

"An' how could it mane anything else?" she asked in answer. "I do be wondering who it is that knife 'll bring us here to-night."

And with that she left the room.

"Mary," said Uncle Dick, as the door closed behind the Careful Katie, "you were remarking that this house was old-fashioned and had no modern conveniences — no dumb-waiter, for example. It seems to me that it has something more useful than a dumb-waiter,—it has a talking waitress."

Mrs. Paulding laughed. "Katie will talk a little too much," she said, "but we don't mind it."

"Mind it!" repeated Uncle Dick. "It is delightful. I enjoy it. I have often heard of a certain person's being a brilliant conversationalist—and I never knew exactly what that meant. But now I know. Why, the Careful Katie is a brilliant conversationalist."

"She 's very good to the pussies," said Polly, as if Uncle Dick were attacking the Careful Katie.

"I 've no doubt she is good in every way," responded Uncle Dick. "She 's a good talker, and that is a good thing. Conversation is her hobby—and we must never look a friend's hobby in the mouth."

In chat like this the evening sped away. Pauline first and then Tom went to bed reluctantly, unwilling to leave their uncle, and fearing that in their absence he might tell of some new and strange adventure by land or sea. The next day was Sunday; and before they went to bed again they had learned more of their uncle's varied career. But it would have taken many a "month of Sundays," as the Careful Katie phrased it, for them to have been told a tithe of the extraordinary adventures in which he had taken part.

Just turned two score years at the time he went back to his sister's house in New York, Richard Rapallo had not spent more than twelve weeks in any one place since he was thirteen. A little before the Rebellion had broken out, in February, 1861, when he was exactly thirteen years old, he had run away to sea. He made a voyage in a whaler as cabin-boy; and when they had gathered a fair harvest of oil and bone in the Northern Pacific, and had come homeward around  the Horn, and were at last almost in sight of port, a terrific storm caught them and blew them far out of their course, and finally wrecked them on Sable Island, that well-filled graveyard of good ships.

When at last Richard Rapallo was taken off in an American vessel, he again met with misfortune, for the ship was captured by the Confederate cruiser "Alabama," then just starting from England on her career of destruction. The American crew saw their ship burnt before their eyes. They were sent off in a little fishing-smack to make their way home as best they could.

Richard Rapallo was only fifteen when he returned to New York and went back to school. He was barely seventeen when he enlisted in the army, then about to make its final effort to crush the Confederate forces and to capture Richmond. It was in January, 1865, that he enlisted; and in February his regiment had its first  skirmish. Taken by surprise, two companies were surrounded and forced to surrender. Richard had scarcely seen any fighting, he had hardly heard a shot fired, but he was taken prisoner like the rest; and a prisoner he remained until the war was over.

Since the surrender of Lee there was hardly anything that

Richard Rapallo had not done; and there was hardly anywhere that he had not been. The restlessness which had led him to run away as a school-boy had grown with the years and with the lack of restraint, until it was quite impossible for him to settle down in any one spot for long.

Young as he was then, only nineteen, he had had charge of an important exhibit at the Paris Exposition of 1867. There he formed friendships which led him to Algiers and thence to Syria and to Egypt. After long wanderings in the Dark Continent he came back to New York again; and he was present at his sister's marriage to his old friend and schoolfellow, Stuyvesant Paulding.

Then again he started out, to the West this time, as if he had had his fill of the East. He had a ranch for a while; and he was in the legislature of Nevada for a term; and he was one of the first men to enter the Black Hills.

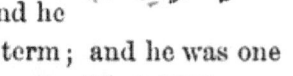

He became interested in a patent for hydraulic mining, and it was to introduce this that he left America for Australia. Here he traveled far into the interior; and he was gone so long with a party of friends that it was feared they had all been lost in the bush.

From Australia he had gone up to China and Japan, and then down again to Calcutta and Bombay, forming one of a party which ascended some of the loftiest peaks of the Himalayas. On his way to Europe he was invited to join an exploring expedition to the antarctic regions; and when the explorations were concluded, it was by one of the ships of this expedition that he was taken to Cape Colony. In time he wandered north to the diamond-mines, and there he had remained nearly a year.

In all his voyages and his journeyings, in the haps and mishaps of his varied career, he had sharpened his shrewdness, mellowed his humor, and broadened his sympathies. There could be no more congenial companion for a healthy and intelligent and inquiring boy like Tom Paulding; and, long before Sunday night, uncle and nephew were on the best of terms.

"I've been 'Jack of all trades,'" said the man to the boy; "I hope you will be master of one. Make your choice early and stick to it, and don't waste your life as I have wasted mine."

Tom wondered whether this could mean that Uncle Dick was not as rich as he and Polly supposed that an uncle ought to be—especially an uncle just back from the diamond-fields.

He was a little reassured on Sunday evening when Uncle Dick brought out a large tarnished pebble, and told them that it was a diamond.

Tom felt that only a rich man could afford to keep diamonds looking as shabby as that.

As to whether he wished his uncle to be rich or not, Tom could not quite determine off-hand. He himself would prefer to find the guineas stolen by Jeffrey Kerr, and with them to pay off the mortgage and make sure his own future and his sister's. But if he did not find the guineas,—and he confessed that he had made no great progress as yet,—then, of course, it would be very convenient indeed to have in the house a wealthy and generous uncle.

Tom went to bed on Sunday night trying to make up his mind whether his uncle was rich, and whether he wanted his uncle to be rich.

Almost the last thing that he heard his uncle say, as he went up to bed that night, made him suspect that perhaps a man might come back from the diamond-fields of South Africa without being enormously wealthy.

What Uncle Dick had said was this: "I've gone abroad on many a cruise, and I've been in many a port,—but my ship has never come home yet." Then Uncle Dick laughed lightly and added, "Perhaps she is now refitting for the voyage—at my castle in Spain."

Tom knew that a castle in Spain was the sole residence of the absolutely homeless, and he thought that this speech meant that his Uncle Dick's having was less than his hope.

On Monday morning, as Tom went off to school, Uncle Dick started with him, saying, "I've two or three things to attend to down-town before I go to see Joshua Hoffmann, and I suppose I'd better start early."

"I can show the way to the elevated railroad station," Tom suggested, as they went down the little flight of steps to the street.

"I don't want any elevated railroad station," replied his uncle. "I'm going to walk. 'Shanks's mare' is my steed:

it does n't take money to make that mare go—but on the other hand it 's true that mare does n't go very far."

Pauline was a little late that morning, and when she came to kiss her mother good-by, before going to school, she could not resist the temptation of the opportunity. She said:

"Marmee, can I ask you a question?"

"Certainly, Polly dear," was the answer.

"It 's about Uncle Dick," Pauline went on, shyly.

"Well?"

"Well, is he very rich?" she asked at last.

Mrs. Paulding looked down at her little daughter and said, "Why do you ask that?"

"Because Tom and I thought that if Uncle Dick had been picking up diamonds—I wonder if they do it in Africa with raw meat and a big bird as they did in 'Sindbad'—if he 'd been finding diamonds, why, of course he was very rich, and he 'd pay the mortgage and make you more comfortable and we 'd all be happier."

"Your Uncle Dick," Mrs. Paulding said, smoothing her daughter's hair, "is not rich. He has very little money, and he has gone now to see Mr. Hoffmann hoping he can get a situation of some sort here in New York."

"Oh!" said Pauline, "then he is poor?"

"Yes," her mother answered. "He is not in need, of course; but he has little or no money."

"I must tell Tom as soon as I can," Pauline remarked, gravely; "and now he has just *got* to find that stolen money at once."

CHAPTER X.

A LESSON IN GEOGRAPHY.

WITHIN forty-eight hours after Mr. Richard Rapallo's arrival at Mrs. Paulding's house, he had made himself quite at home there. He took his place in the family circle easily and unobtrusively, and before he had been in the house more than a week, Pauline found herself wondering how they had ever got on without Uncle Dick; Tom recognized in his uncle the wise friend for whom he had been longing of late; Mrs. Paulding was very glad to have her brother with her again; and even the Careful Katie was pleased.

"It's a sight for sore eyes," she said, "to see Mrs. Paulding so cheerful! And Mr. Richard was always a lively boy and kept the pot a-boilin'."

In the Careful Katie Uncle Dick took amused interest. Her willingness to enter now and then into the talk at the dinner-table afforded him unending entertainment. He usually called her the "Brilliant Conversationalist"; and as he knew that this was a nickname she would not understand, he did not hesitate to allude to the Brilliant Conversationalist even when Katie was actually present.

He delighted in drawing her out and in getting at the strange superstitions in which she believed, for they came up in the most unexpected ways. He would set Pauline to lead her on about signs and warnings. Having been told that the dropping of a knife meant the coming of a "beau" or of "some other gentleman," and that the dropping of a fork indicated the visit of a lady, he was greatly puzzled to know what the dropping of a spoon could portend. Pauline agreed to find out for him.

Pauline and her uncle were great friends. He had become interested in her and in her doings at once, and he had the art of seeing things as she did. In time she wholly forgot that there was a great difference of years between them, and she came to talk with her uncle as with a comrade of her own age.

She reported that the fall of a spoon foretold that "it" was coming — "it" being something vague, unknown, impossible to predict with precision.

"I see," said Uncle Dick, when Polly told him this. "I see it all now. The scheme is as simple and as logical as one could wish. The knife indicates that the coming visitor is masculine, while the fork is the feminine of this prediction, and the spoon is the neuter."

"So it is!" Polly declared, with surprise. "It's just like the grammar, then, is n't it? And I think grammar is horrid!"

A LESSON IN GEOGRAPHY.

"There is n't much English grammar left nowadays," Uncle Dick returned. "We have shaken off most of the unnecessary distinctions of more complicated languages. In French, now, the sun is masculine, while in German it is feminine."

"Then, if I was a French-and-German girl I should n't know whether the sun was a man or a woman?" asked Polly. "I think that would be terrible!"

"It would be terrible indeed," Uncle Dick answered, gravely; "but perhaps the sun would still shine, even if you did n't know its gender."

"Grammar 's bad enough," continued the little girl, "but sometimes I think joggraphy 's worse."

"Oh, it 's joggraphy still, is it?" asked her uncle. "It used to be when I was a boy at school."

"Of course it 's joggraphy," she returned, in surprise. "What could it be?"

"I did n't know," Uncle Dick responded. "I thought that perhaps it might now be geography."

"Oh, Uncle Dick!" said Polly, blushing, "I think it 's real mean of you to catch me like that." Then, after a little pause, she added, "We do say joggraphy, I know—that is, we generally shorten it to jog. We shorten everything we can. We say Am. hist. for American history, and comp. for compositions, and rith. for arithmetic."

"I suppose that you have to condense a great deal," Uncle Dick remarked, gravely, "because you have so little time before you."

Pauline did not see the irony of this. She went on gaily: "I don't like jog. any more; we are in Africa now—"

"I should n't have thought it, from the weather here," Uncle Dick interrupted, glancing at the window, through which he could see the falling flakes of the first snow-storm of the winter.

"I mean we are in Africa in our jog.," she explained.

"I see," he answered, sedately.

"And I don't like it at all. It's all so hard and so—so dry."

"I've found Africa very dry myself," admitted her uncle.

"Have you been there?" she asked. Then she added hastily, "Why, of course you have. You were at the diamond-fields. Now, is n't that funny? I read about the diamond-fields in my jog., and it never struck me that they were real places, you know, where real people might be, as you were."

Uncle Dick laughed a little. "I can understand that," he remarked. "They were simply a name on the map—simply something that you had to study out of a book—not something interesting, and alive, where there are men and women and children. Well, I'll try and make you take a little more interest in that name on the map."

Then he lifted her on his knee and told her about the diamond-fields. He described the country thereabouts and the difficulties of the journey there. He explained how the mines were worked, and he showed her that the laborers there were human beings with good qualities and bad qualities of their own. He set before her in a few graphic words the different nationalities that are to be found in South Africa—the English colonists, the Dutch settlers, and the native Africans.

When he had come to an end of his description, Pauline

UNCLE DICK TELLS POLLY ABOUT THE DIAMOND-FIELDS.

kissed him and said, "Uncle, I shall never hate jog. again. I had no idea it was so interesting. And besides, when we have a review now, I shall know ever so much more than any of the other girls. I shall surprise them so!"

Uncle Dick smiled again. "I've had that feeling myself," he confessed. "When I went back to school after I'd been on a voyage, geography was my favorite lesson, because I'd seen so many of the places. I remember to this day how conceited I was when I told them all that it was n't necessary to go around Cape Horn if you could get into the Strait of Lemaire."

"I'll remember that, too," Polly declared, promptly.

"As long as we were at work on South America," continued Uncle Dick, "I was all right. I'd been around it, and I thought I knew all about it; and of course I had seen more than any of the others. But pride had a fall at last, and conceit got knocked on the head as soon as we finished America and began on Europe."

"Had n't you been to Europe?" she inquired.

"Not then; I did n't cross the Atlantic until '67, at the time of the Paris Exposition. And as I knew, or thought I knew, all about South America, I'd got into the habit of not studying my geography lesson. There were times when I did n't even open the book. So one day,—I can remember now how the school looked when the teacher asked me the question,—it was late in June, and we were all restless. I think the teacher saw this and wished to make it as easy for us as she could, so she called on me. She had found out that I liked to talk, and that the other boys liked to hear me because I used to bring in words and phrases I'd picked up from the sailor-men during our long voyage. So she called, 'Rapallo,' and I stood up. And she asked, 'Which way does the Nile flow?' Now, I did n't know anything at all about the Nile or about Africa, and I was at a loss. I hesitated, and I tried to remember how the Nile looked on the map. But I had n't really studied the map, and I could n't remember anything at all. So I did n't know what to say. I stood there foolishly, thinking as hard as I could. Then I tried to get out of it by luck or else by sheer guessing. So when she repeated the question, 'What is the course of the Nile?' I answered boldly, 'Southwest by south.' And you should have heard how the boys laughed! The teacher had to join in too."

And Uncle Dick himself laughed heartily at the recollection of his blunder.

Pauline smiled, a little doubtfully.

"I think I 'll go out and get a taste of that snow-storm," said her uncle, rising. "It is the first I 've seen in three years."

As soon as Uncle Dick had left the house, Pauline went to her own room and got down her geography and turned to the map of Africa. She wished to make sure of her own knowledge as to the course of the Nile, so that she could enjoy her uncle's blunder.

CHAPTER XI.

SANTA CLAUS BRINGS A SUGGESTION.

THE snow-storm kept up all night, and in the morning there was no denying that winter had come at last. The steep slopes of the Riverside Park were covered three inches deep. The boys got out their sleds and began to coast. A sharp frost followed the snow-storm and froze the water out of the snow, so that it was too dry to make into balls.

Before the Christmas vacation began, the aspect of the landscape had undergone its winter change. The skies were dull and gray, though the frosty sunset glowed ruddy over the Jersey hills. Ice began to form in the river; the night-boats had ceased running weeks before; and now the long tows of canal-boats were seen no more. Even the heavy freight-boats and the impudent little tugs became infrequent, as if they feared to be caught in the ice. The long freight-trains stood still on the tracks of the railroad down by the water's edge, or moved slowly past as the powerful locomotives puffed their white steam into the clear cold air.

Uncle Dick was in and out of the house in the most irregular way. Generally he went out early in the morning, and sometimes he did not return till late at night. Mrs. Paulding never delayed dinner in the hope of his coming back in time for it. He had told her not to expect him until she saw him.

"I've many things to do," he explained, "and I've many people to see, and sometimes I have to catch them on the jump, when I get the chance."

Just what his business was he never explained. He did not tell any one in the house whether or not he had succeeded in securing the situation for which he had applied to Joshua Hoffmann. Pauline was very curious, and she wanted to ask her uncle about this; but she thought it would not be polite. She was always glad when Uncle Dick "took an afternoon off," as he phrased it, for then he was likely to spend a good part of it talking to her.

Tom had been busy with the examinations at school and with the preparations for Christmas at home, so that it was not until the vacation began that he found an opportunity to consult his uncle about the lost guineas.

On the afternoon before Christmas, Tom went out to give an order for the supplies his mother needed to meet an unexpected demand for several kinds of cake which a tardy customer of the Woman's Exchange had called for. Having done his errand, he turned into the Riverside Drive and began to walk along the parapet.

When he came near the handsome house which Mr. Joshua

Hoffmann had recently built, he saw a carriage stop before the door. Two gentlemen got out, and the carriage drove around the corner to the stable. One of these gentlemen was tall, thin, white-haired, and evidently very old, although he still carried himself erect. The other was Tom's Uncle Dick.

The old gentleman apparently asked Mr. Rapallo to enter the house, and Uncle Dick declined, shaking hands and bidding good-by. The elderly man went up the few steps which took him inside his own grounds; then he paused and called Mr. Rapallo back. Leaning over the low stone wall which surrounded his lawn, the old gentleman had a brief talk with Uncle Dick — a talk which ended a little before Tom came opposite to them.

Then the elderly man again shook hands with Mr. Rapallo and went into the house.

As Uncle Dick turned he caught sight of Tom Paulding.

"Hullo, youngster!" he cried across the road. "Don't you want to go for a walk?"

It seemed as if Uncle Dick could never have enough walking. Tom thought sometimes that his uncle took long tramps just to humor his restlessness — to "let off steam," as Tom expressed it.

Mr. Rapallo crossed the road and joined Tom. "Where shall we go?" he asked.

"Are you in a hurry?" Tom inquired.

"I'm never in a hurry," he answered.

"I mean, have you time for a long talk with me?" was Tom's next question.

MR. JOSHUA HOFFMANN HAS A TALK WITH UNCLE DICK.

"Of course I have," he replied. "We've all the time there is."

"Then I'll take you up and show you the place where my great-grandfather was robbed," said Tom, as they dropped into the steady pace at which Mr. Rapallo always walked. "I've been wanting to tell you all about it and to get your advice."

"Advice is inexpensive," laughed his uncle; "there is n't anything I can afford to give more freely. But I'm afraid you ll not find it a very substantial Christmas present."

"You see, Uncle," Tom pursued, eagerly, "I've worked on this now till I've done all I can. I've got to the end of my rope, and I thought that you could help me out with your experience."

"I've had plenty of experience, too," returned Uncle Dick. "If experience was an available stock in trade, I could fit up a store and sell off my surplus supply. I've more than I need for my own use. I've been pretty nearly everywhere, and I've seen all sorts of things, and I've met all sorts of people, and—I've nothing to show for it now but experience."

"Your not having money does n't make you miserable, anyway," said Tom.

"I'm richer than anybody I ever met," Uncle Dick declared, seriously.

Tom looked at him in surprise.

"I don't mean in mere money," he went on. "Money is only one of the standards by which you measure riches—and it is n't a very good one, either. I'm rich because I have all

I want. I've met wealthy men in all parts of the world—in New York and in New Zealand, among the Eskimos and among the Arabs; they had different ideas of wealth, of course, but they were all alike in one thing—they all wanted more. I've never met a very wealthy man who did n't want more than he had. Now, I don't. I'm content. And that's 'the best gift of heaven to man'—contentment. It takes few things to give it. Health, first, of course; then freedom; then food and clothing; after that, a roof over one's head and a fire if it is cold. I've been in places where clothing and fire and shelter were not needed, and where the food grew wild for the picking. In those places a man can get the essentials of life very easily. But however he may get them, the main thing is to be content with little. After all, I believe contentment is a habit. So I advise you to get accustomed to being content as soon as you can. Then you will never long to change places with a wealthy man. With most of them, the more they have the more they want. I was talking just now with a very wealthy man—"

"The Old Gentleman who leaned over the Wall?" Tom inquired.

"The Old Gentleman who leaned over the Wall," his uncle assented. "He has money, houses, lands, mines, ships; but though he is old and has now earned his rest, and though the care of all these things wears on him, still he wants more. He is a good man, too,—one of the best men in the world to-day,—and probably he wishes for more money only that he may do more good with it. But he does wish for it, all the same."

"I'm afraid I'm not so content as you, Uncle Dick," said Tom. "I want more than I have. You know mother is troubled about that mortgage, and I'd like to go to the School of Mines, and I think Pauline ought to have a chance, too; so that's why I'm trying to find the gold which was stolen from my great-grandfather."

"It's a boy's habit to be hopeful and striving," Uncle Dick replied. "I should not wish you to look at the world with my eyes yet a while. But even when you are trying for what you think would better you—even then you can be content with what you actually have. Now tell me all about this gold which vanished suddenly and was seen no more."

Tom began at the beginning and told Uncle Dick the whole story. He took Mr. Rapallo over the ground, and showed the exact position of the two armies on the night of the robbery. He had in his pocket the map Nicholas Paulding had roughly outlined. With the aid of this he traced for Uncle Dick the course of the little stream which had separated the hostile camps the night before the battle, and he pointed out the stepping-stones by means of which a passage might have been had from one bank to the other. He gave Mr. Rapallo all the information he had been able to extract from the papers gathered by Wyllys Paulding. He explained all the circumstances of Jeffrey Kerr's taking the bags containing the two thousand guineas, and of his escape with them. He dwelt on the fact that after the second sentinel had fired on Kerr, the thief had never been seen again, so far as anybody knew.

"In other words," said Uncle Dick, "this man Kerr took the money, ran outside our lines, and then vanished."

"That's it exactly," Tom replied.

"And when he vanished, the gold disappeared too," Mr. Rapallo continued. "You are right in calling this a puzzle. It is a puzzle of the most puzzling kind."

"And there is one question which puzzles me quite as much as the fate of the thief or the disappearance of the gold," Tom declared; "and that's why it was that my grandfather suddenly gave up the search."

"That is odd," Uncle Dick confessed; "very odd, indeed. It will bear a good deal of thinking over."

"And I want you to help me, Uncle Dick," pleaded Tom.

"Of course I will," replied Mr. Rapallo, heartily. "I'll do what I can—that is, if I can do anything. Have you told any of the boys here about this?"

"They know I'm going to try to find it," Tom replied, "but that's all they do know. I thought at first of consulting Harry Zachary,—he has such good ideas. He's just been reading a book called the 'Last Days of Pompeii,' and he wants us to make a big volcano for the Fourth of July and have an eruption of Vesuvius after it gets dark, and then by the light of the burning mountain two of us will fight a duel with stilettos—that's a kind of Italian bowie-knife, is n't it?"

"Yes," answered Uncle Dick, smiling. "I think that is a good scheme. This young friend of yours seems to have excellent ideas, as you say. Why did n't you consult him?"

"Well," Tom answered, "his head 's all right, but he is n't very strong, and he gets scared easily. Besides, his father thinks he 's delicate, and he won't always let him out. His father 's a tailor—that is, he manufactures clothes. Harry says he has more than a hundred hands."

"Quite a Briareus," said Mr. Rapallo. "And is he the only one you could take into confidence?"

"Oh, no," Tom responded; "there 's Cissy Smith."

"I don't think I would advise you to consult a girl," said his uncle.

"Cissy is n't a girl," Tom explained. "'Cissy' is simply short for Cicero. His full name is Marcus Cicero Smith, Junior."

"Then I think I must know his father," Mr. Rapallo declared; "that is, if he 's a doctor, and if he used to live in Denver."

"He did," said Tom.

"And why did n't you consult him?" asked his uncle.

"Well," Tom explained, a little hesitatingly, "I don't know that I can tell, for sure. I like Cissy. He 's my best friend. But he 's so sharp, and he sits down on one so hard. And besides, I thought I 'd rather do all the work myself."

They were then walking along the upper terrace of Morningside Park.

Mr. Rapallo glanced down into the park below and said, "Is n't that boy making signals to you?"

Tom leaned over and caught sight of Corkscrew Lott, who was waving his hands as if signaling.

As Tom came to the edge of the parapet, Lott whistled:

Tom promptly answered:

"That sounds like a rallying-call," said Mr. Rapallo, smiling.

"We 've got a secret society, called the Black Band, and that 's our signal," Tom explained.

They walked a little way down toward Lott, and stood still until he came up. Then Tom presented him to Mr. Rapallo.

Lott hardly waited for this introduction, he was so anxious to communicate his intelligence.

"Have you heard the news?" he asked, twisting with impatience.

"What news?" Tom returned.

"Then you have n't heard it," Lott went on, gleefully. "It was found only this forenoon, and I was almost the first to see it."

"What was found?" asked Tom, with a sudden chill as he feared that possibly some one else had discovered the treasure he was after.

"It 's the skeleton of a soldier who was killed during the Revolutionary War," Lott explained.

Uncle Dick and Tom looked at each other with the same thought in their minds.

"CORKSCREW" TELLS UNCLE DICK AND TOM OF THE DISCOVERY BY THE AQUEDUCT LABORERS.

SANTA CLAUS BRINGS A SUGGESTION.

"Where was this discovered?" Mr. Rapallo asked.

"Over there," Corkscrew answered, pointing toward the Hudson River behind them. "The men at work there on the new aqueduct dug up the bones. It was the skeleton of a British soldier."

"A British soldier?" echoed Mr. Rapallo. "How do you know that?"

"Oh, everybody says so," Lott answered. "Besides, they found things with him that prove it."

"Did they find any money?" cried Tom, anxiously.

"Did n't they though?" Corkscrew replied.

Again Tom and Uncle Dick exchanged glances, and their faces fell.

"Do you know how much they found?" inquired Mr. Rapallo.

"Of course I do," Corkscrew answered. "I went up at once, and I asked all about it, and I 've seen all the money. There are two silver shillings and a silver sixpence and a copper penny — a great big one with the head of George the Second on it."

"Is that all?" Tom demanded.

"Is n't that enough?" Lott returned. "How much do you think a British soldier ought to have had?"

Tom drew a breath of relief. "If that is all," he began —

"How do you know it was a British soldier?" Mr. Rapallo repeated. "An American soldier might have had two-and-six in silver and a penny in copper."

"The money was n't all that was found," Lott explained.

"I thought you said it was," Tom interrupted.

"I did n't say anything of the sort," Lott replied. "I said that was all the money; but they found something else — the buttons of his uniform; and Dr. Smith, who has collected buttons — I 'm going to begin a collection at once; I can get one from a 'sparrow' policeman, and I 've a cousin in the fire department at Boston, and — "

"Never mind about the collection you are going to begin," said Mr. Rapallo; "tell us about these buttons now."

"Well," Lott returned, "Dr. Smith recognized them at once; he said that they were worn in 1776 by the Seventeenth Light Dragoons; and that that was one of the British regiments which took part in the Battle of Harlem Heights."

"And what did Dr. Smith say about the death of the poor fellow whose bones have been found?" asked Uncle Dick.

"He said it was easy to see how the man had been killed, and he took a big musket-ball out of the skull," said Lott. "He thinks that in the hurry of the fighting some of the other soldiers must have thrown a little earth hastily over the body, and left it where it fell; and so, in time, with the washing of the rain and the settling of the dust and the growing of the grass, somehow the skeleton got to be well under ground. Why, it was at least six feet down, where they dug it out."

"Are you sure that they did not find anything else with it?" Mr. Rapallo inquired.

"Certain sure!" said Corkscrew. "I asked every one of them all about it. Oh, that 's all right: if there 'd been anything else, I 'd have found out all about it. Maybe the men are there still; you can go and ask them yourself, and I can show you exactly where the bones were."

Mr. Rapallo and Tom Paulding walked with Lott to the place where the men were yet at work sinking a deep ditch for one of the huge pipes of the new aqueduct. The laborers had advanced at least ten feet beyond the spot in which the skeleton had been discovered, but Corkscrew pointed out the place.

Uncle Dick asked the foreman a few questions, and then he and Tom started for home.

"I don't see how that can be the skeleton of your thief, Tom," said Mr. Rapallo, as they walked on after parting with Lott.

"I 'm sure that Kerr could n't have got to the place where those bones were found," Tom declared. "Kerr did n't reach the British camp, and that place is well inside their lines. Besides, he could n't have had on the uniform of the Seventeenth Light Dragoons, you know; he was an assistant paymaster in our army. And then those two shillings, and that sixpence, and that penny — there was more than that in my great-grandfather's money-bags! No; this can't be the man we 're after."

"Then you are no nearer the solution of your problem," said Uncle Dick. "I 'm afraid it will take you a long while to work it out. I 'd help you if I could, but I don't see how I can."

"It helps me just to have some one to talk to about it," Tom urged.

"Oh, you can talk to me till you are tired," Uncle Dick laughed. "The mystery of the thing fascinates me, and I shall be glad to talk about it. But you will have to do the hard thinking yourself. 'Be sure you're right—then go ahead!' That was a good motto for Davy Crockett, and it is n't a bad one for any other American."

"I wish I only knew which way to go," said Tom; "I'd go ahead with all my might."

"Put on your thinking-cap," remarked Mr. Rapallo, as they mounted the flight of steps leading from the street to the knoll on which stood Mrs. Paulding's house. "Sleep on it. To-morrow is Christmas, you know; perhaps in the morning you will find an idea in your stocking."

Generally Tom was a late sleeper, like most boys, and it was not easy to rouse him from his slumbers. But on Christmas morning, by some strange chance, he waked very early. Despite his utmost endeavor he could not go to sleep again. He lay there wide awake, and he recalled the events of the preceding day. Soon he began to turn over in his mind the circumstances connected with Jeffrey Kerr's mysterious disappearance.

Suddenly he sprang from his bed and lighted the gas. Without waiting to dress, he pulled out the box of papers and searched among them for a certain newspaper. When he had found this he read a marked paragraph with almost feverish eagerness. Then he put the paper away again in the box, and dressed himself as rapidly as he could.

By the time he got down-stairs, creeping softly that he might not disturb his mother, it was just daybreak.

At the foot of the stairs he met the Careful Katie, who was just back from early mass.

"Holy Saints defend us!" she cried. "Is that the boy, or his banshee?"

"Merry Christmas, Katie!" he said, as he put on his overcoat.

"An' is it goin' out ye are?" she asked in astonishment. "For why? Ye can't buy no more Christmas presents— the stores is n't open, even them that ain't closed the day."

"I 've got to go out to see about something," he explained. "I shall be back in half an hour."

"It 'll bring no luck this goin' out in the night, an' not to church either," said the Careful Katie, as she opened the door for him.

An hour or so later, when Mr. Rapallo was dressing leisurely, there came a tap at his door.

"Who 's there?" he cried.

"Merry Christmas, Uncle Dick!" Tom answered. "You were right, and Santa Claus has given me a suggestion."

"What do you mean?" asked his uncle, opening the door.

"I have found an idea in my stocking," Tom explained; "or at least it came to me this morning early, and I 've been out to see about it. And I think I 've made a discovery."

"Produce your discovery!" Uncle Dick responded, noting the excitement in the boy's voice and the light in his eyes.

"I think I know what became of Jeffrey Kerr," said Tom; "and if I 'm right, then I know where the stolen gold is!"

CHAPTER XII.

THE FATE OF JEFFREY KERR.

NCLE DICK looked at Tom for a moment Then he whistled gently.

"If you have found out that, then you have the finest Christmas present of us all."

"I think I have," Tom declared.

"I'm very glad to hear it," his uncle responded, heartily. "Now, sit down here and tell me all about it."

Tom took a chair and sat down beside Mr. Rapallo.

"I think I know where the thief is," the boy began, "and I hope I know where the gold is; though, of course, I'm not sure. After all, it is only a guess, but still—"

"If you express all your doubts before you let me have all the facts," interrupted Uncle Dick, "it will be a long time before I can see what you are driving at. Better begin at the beginning."

"The real beginning," Tom answered, "was when I got to looking at this mystery just as if it was a problem in algebra. Jeffrey Kerr was my x. He wasn't exactly an unknown quantity, but there was a lot about him I did n't know. I set down the facts, and then tried to work out my x — that is, to see what had become of Kerr. If what my grandfather

"'I THINK I KNOW WHERE THE THIEF IS,' THE BOY BEGAN."

had found out and written down was right, then the thief had vanished suddenly after he had got past the sentries of Washington's army. Now, this morning when I was waking up I found that I was thinking about this problem, just as if

I had been at work on it in my sleep, puzzling it out in a dream. I was still half asleep when I found that one thought kept on coming back and coming back. And I suppose that thought was the present Santa Claus had brought me during the night, as you said he would."

"I did n't say that he would, for sure," said Mr. Rapallo. "I hoped that perhaps he might. What was it that he told you?"

"It seems so simple," Tom continued, "that I don't see how I ever came to miss seeing it for so long."

"The greatest ideas are generally the simplest," Uncle Dick remarked, encouragingly. "You remember that little egg trick of Columbus's?"

"And it never seemed to me quite fair either," Tom returned, "because—"

"Don't let 's discuss that now," his uncle interposed. "What was your new idea?"

"Well," Tom went on, "I found myself thinking that as Kerr had left the American army, and as he had n't got to the British army, and as he had n't ever been seen anywhere since that night, or heard of by anybody,—why, perhaps the shot the sentinel had fired at him had wounded him badly—you remember my great-grandfather's account said there was a cry of pain after that second shot?"

"I remember," said Uncle Dick.

"And if the shot had wounded him badly," Tom continued, "that perhaps he had fallen dead somewhere between the lines, and that perhaps somehow his body had got covered over or concealed or something of that sort, and so it might perhaps be there now."

"I understand," Mr. Rapallo remarked, as Tom paused for a moment to see if his uncle were following him. "If the body was hidden then, there is no reason why it might not be there to this day. But where can it be hidden? That will be a difficult question to solve."

Tom smiled cheerfully. "Well," he said, "of course I don't know that I 've found out that, certain sure; but I 've got another idea about that, too."

"Produce idea number two!" ordered Uncle Dick.

"As soon as I had really got hold of the first idea—the one that possibly Kerr was wounded by that shot and that his body might be there now—I waked right up," Tom responded; "and it was when I was wide awake that I wondered where we could look for Kerr's body, with the gold on it, perhaps. Suddenly it struck me that as Kerr was trying to escape to the British, and as he knew the country,—he 'd been living up near here at an old mill for months before,— why, he 'd naturally try some kind of a short cut. There was a little brook separating those two camps, and it had been raining hard all day,—I looked at the old newspaper to make sure of that, but I believe it nearly always does rain hard after there 's been a battle,—and so I thought the brook would be high, and Kerr was smart enough to know that it would be, and so perhaps he 'd make for those stepping-stones. You remember, I once showed them to you marked on the map my great-grandfather made?"

"Yes, I remember," Mr. Rapallo replied; "and I think I see where you are going. I should n't wonder if you were on the right track at last."

Tom's eyes lighted again with pleasure as he continued:

"I got out that map, and I looked to see if it would help me. Well, the place is marked where the first sentry stood that fired at Kerr, and then the place is marked where the second sentry stood when *he* fired; so I drew a line from one to the other, and I thought that would show which way Kerr was going. Then I stretched out that line toward the British troops to see where he would cross the brook; and I found that if he had kept on the same way he started, then he was running straight for those stepping-stones which my great-grandfather had marked in his plan."

"And supposing you are right?" Uncle Dick queried.

"Supposing I'm right," Tom responded, "and supposing he was badly wounded, perhaps when he got to those stepping-stones and tried to cross, he slipped and fell in. You see the brook was up, and maybe the water was over the top of some of the stones. It was a very dark night, and he was running for his life, and perhaps he slipped and fell into the pool."

"Well?" said Mr. Rapallo.

"Well, if he did," Tom went on — "if he did fall, and he was wounded, and the current was strong, and he had all that heavy gold weighing him down, perhaps he was drowned there."

"If that happened," Uncle Dick inquired, "why was n't the body found next day?"

"I thought," Tom suggested, "that perhaps the strength of the current might have rolled the body into the deepest part of the pool, and then the sand and dirt and things which the brook was carrying down would be caught by the body; and perhaps there would be enough of them to cover it up completely. And if there was, why, then perhaps the gold is there now."

"With the skeleton of the thief guarding it for you," said Mr. Rapallo.

"What do you think about this idea?" Tom asked, anxiously.

"I think," his uncle replied, "that you are probably right. I see that your story has a 'perhaps' in almost every sentence. Perhaps the man was wounded, perhaps he tried to cross at the stepping-stones, perhaps he slipped, perhaps he was drowned partly by the weight of the guineas he had stolen, perhaps the brook washed down sand and earth enough to cover him, and perhaps nobody has ever found him. Here are *perhapses* enough and to spare, you must admit."

As his uncle paused, Tom's face fell. This did not seem so cordial an acquiescence as he had hoped for.

"But your theory at least fits all the facts as we know them," said Mr. Rapallo, cheerfully. "It seems to me excellent as a 'working hypothesis,' so to speak. At least it may very well explain the mystery of Kerr's disappearance. And if I were you I should go ahead on this line, and fight it out if it takes all winter."

"Will you help me?" asked Tom, eagerly.

"Of course I will," his uncle responded, heartily. "Whatever I can do, I will. First of all, have you any idea where the current would have taken the body of the thief?"

"Yes," Tom answered, quickly; "I think I know—at least I've been guessing at it. On the map the pool is shaped somewhat like a figure eight, with the stepping-stones at the middle in the narrow part, and with the lower end swung on one side in a sort of bay; and the brook goes on out of one corner of this sort of bay. Now, it seems to me that if Kerr slipped off the stepping-stones, he probably rolled to the middle of this lower pool—and that he is there now."

"Do you think that any one else has found his body?" asked Uncle Dick.

"No," said Tom. "At least I think nobody has ever thought of digging there. The brook has dried up only since they began to open the streets through here. I showed you where the stepping-stones are, and the little pool just below them is still to be traced out—at least I can do it now I've seen the map. The trouble is that the pool is in a vacant block which they have begun to fill in. The lots are 'way down below the level of the street. They've done some filling in, and they are going to do more soon. I went there to see it just now, and I think I could see the edge of the pool distinctly. But the part where I guessed the guineas were has been filled in twenty feet at least."

"Does a street run across it?" Mr. Rapallo inquired. "Foolish people used to think that the streets of great cities were paved with gold; and it would be curious if there were really treasure hidden down below their surfaces."

"This is n't a street," Tom explained; "it 's just the ordinary filling in, with rubbish and dirt and old brickbats and ashes and things. It starts about the middle of the block and makes a sort of bow-window into the middle of the vacant lots."

"Then how are you going to get out the golden guineas?" asked Uncle Dick.

"That 's just what I don't know," Tom answered. "I 'm counting on you to help me out there."

"I 've mined for gold in California, and for silver in the Black Hills, and for diamonds in South Africa," Mr. Rapallo replied, with an amused smile; "but I never supposed that I should sink a shaft in the streets of New York in search of buried treasure. It will be a novel experience, at any rate. But we must see what we can do. This afternoon, if you will take me over to the place where the pool was, I 'll have a look around."

Tom arose to go. When he had opened the door he hesitated and then said: "If you don't mind, Uncle Dick, I 'd rather we did n't say anything about this 'working hypothesis' until we know whether it will work or not."

"Certainly not," Mr. Rapallo replied. "It is always best to say nothing till you have something to show. 'When in doubt, hold your tongue'— there 's a good motto."

Then he came out into the hall to Tom, and they went down-stairs together to their Christmas breakfast.

CHAPTER XIII.

CHRISTMAS MORNING AND CHRISTMAS NIGHT.

N Mrs. Paulding's family it was the tradition to keep Christmas and to make presents; but the moderate circumstances of the household prevented the purchase of costly gifts. Nor was the preparation of presents made by the giver allowed to become burdensome. There are homes where the pressure of Christmas giving has crushed out the proper Christmas feeling,—where the obligation is accepted of providing every other member of the household with a present which is often useless and which is always expensive. Nothing of this sort was seen at Mrs. Paulding's fireside. With gentle tact she found out early in the fall what were the cherished desires of her children; and, in so far as her means might allow, she gratified these at Christmas. They in turn consulted each other and saved up their pocket-money that they might give her something likely to be useful.

On this Christmas morning there was the added interest of Uncle Dick's being in the house. Just what to give him had greatly puzzled Tom and Polly, but they had at last hit upon things they thought their uncle would welcome. Polly made him a "housewife" to contain needles and thread and buttons and tapes, and a tiny pair of scissors.

She explained to Tom that if Uncle Dick ever went back to South Africa, or even out West again among those Indians, she thought the needles and the other accompanying tools of woman's craft might be very useful.

"If the real Africans," she said, "are anything like the pictures in my jog., I don't believe that Uncle Dick could find one of them to do his sewing for him. They can't have had much practice in making buttonholes. If those pictures are right, then I should n't wonder if there was n't a single sewing-machine in all South Africa. So, you see, he might have to mend his own clothes some day and sew on buttons Of course he's only a man and he would n't do it well; but, all the same, I think he ought not to go away again without needle and thread."

Mr. Rapallo had told them that he never knew how long he would be able to stay with them. He might, at any time, be called away suddenly; and if he once went, he could not guess when he should get back.

Tom had borne in mind this possibility of his uncle's traveling, and he had gone over to Cissy Smith's, whose father had given him a lathe the year before; and with Cissy's assistance Tom had turned a box large enough to hold a few of the indispensable effects of a traveler.

When Tom and his uncle came down that Christmas morning, they found Mrs. Paulding and Pauline waiting for them at the breakfast-table; and the presents were placed at the plate of each member of the household.

Mrs. Paulding was always pleased with what her children gave her; and she had interpreted their desires so sympathetically that they were sure to be delighted with her presents to them.

Uncle Dick thanked Pauline for the housewife and Tom for the box.

"What do you suppose I have for you?" he asked. Perhaps he had noticed a slight shadow of disappointment on their faces when they failed to find by their plates any gift from him.

"I don't know," said Tom, interested in the presents in spite of his excitement over his "working hypothesis" as to the whereabouts of the stolen guineas.

"But I'm sure it will be simply lovely," volunteered Pauline.

"Well," said Uncle Dick, "for a long while I could not find out what any of you wanted; but at last I heard Polly say that she wished she was rich enough to buy her mother a sewing-machine, because there were so many things she wanted to make for herself. So I have got a sewing-machine for Polly; it is now upstairs in her room."

"Oh, Uncle!" cried Polly. "Thank you ever so much!" and she jumped from her chair and ran around and kissed him.

"And one day," Uncle Dick resumed, "when Tom and I

were walking by the water, I heard him say that he wished he had a telescope to look up and down the stream. Now, a telescope is not so useful as a field-glass; and if Tom will look under his chair he will find a field-glass through which he can see a good many miles up the Hudson."

After Tom had thanked him, Mr. Rapallo turned to his sister and said, "The present I hoped to have for you, Mary, is not ready yet. I may have it by New Year's—and I may have to go after it. But I think you will like it when you get it, and—"

"I am sure I shall, Richard," was Mrs. Paulding's response.

"And until you do get it," Uncle Dick continued, "I sha'n't tell you anything at all about it."

"But—" Polly began, with a keen disappointment depicted in her face.

"*But*," her uncle interrupted, "you will have to possess your soul in patience, for I shall not give you a hint about it until you see it."

"An' quite right, too," said the Brilliant Conversationalist, who was bringing in the buckwheat cakes. "The child may be sure that whatever you buy, Mr. Richard, will be beautiful. See what I found in me kitchen this mornin'"; and she produced a pair of rather startling ear-rings that Uncle Dick had bought for her.

After breakfast they all went to church; and after dinner Uncle Dick called Tom and took him off for a walk.

"I want you to show me the place where you think Jeffrey Kerr lies buried, with the gold he stole from your great-grandfather concealed about his skeleton," he said, as they started out.

Tom led him straight to the vacant lots, into which from about the middle of the block a tongue of made land projected.

"There's where the stepping-stones were, according to this map," said Tom, as he handed the paper to his uncle. "That big boulder there used to be one of them, I think; and as far as I can make out, those two other high rocks over there belonged to them, too."

It took Mr. Rapallo but a short time to familiarize himself with the ground before him and to identify it with that sketched out in the rough but fairly accurate map which he held in his hand. As yet there was hardly a house within two or three blocks on either side; and in one of the adjoining blocks also, below the street-level, it was not difficult to trace the course of the brook, partly by the stones and partly by the stumps of the broken willows which had lined its banks here and there. The outline of the pool below the stepping-stones was less easy to make out, but at last Mr. Rapallo and Tom were able to identify its limits to their satisfaction.

"Where do you think the deep part of the pool was?" asked Uncle Dick.

"Here," said Tom, as he pointed to a stone which projected a little from the edge of the peninsula of filled land. "I think that is the tip of a tall rock marked in the map; and if it is, then the deep part of the pool was just behind that."

CHRISTMAS MORNING AND CHRISTMAS NIGHT. 143

"That is to say," his uncle rejoined, "if the body of Jeffrey Kerr is here at all, it is buried somewhere near the base of that stone?"

"Yes," Tom answered; "don't you think so?"

"I think your enthusiasm is catching," Uncle Dick replied; "and now I am here on the spot, I begin to believe that the stolen gold is down there somewhere, almost under our feet. By the way, how far down do you suppose it is?"

"I've been thinking about that," Tom returned, "and I believe that the skeleton must be several feet below the level of the bottom of the old pool, as it is now — perhaps only a foot or so, and perhaps three or four."

"And the part of the pool near the rock there is buried under at least ten feet of dirt, ashes, and all sorts of builder's rubbish. It won't be easy for us to excavate this to prospect for that gold."

"Suppose we go down and look at it," Tom suggested.

His uncle started down the steep incline and the boy followed. At the point where the rock stood, the level of the lot was fully twenty feet below the surface of the street; and farther down, nearer the river, it sloped away still deeper. In the hollows here and there the snow lingered, dry and harsh beneath their feet. The ground was frozen hard.

"There is no use in our trying to do anything here until there is a thaw," Mr. Rapallo declared. "In fact, I think that it will be best to postpone our serious effort to excavate until spring."

"And when spring comes will you be here, Uncle Dick?" Tom asked, eagerly.

"That's more than I can say, Tom," he answered. "It depends — well, it depends on many things."

"And in spring how are we going to dig out all that dirt?" Tom inquired.

"I don't know how we shall do it," Mr. Rapallo replied. "But you will find a way out of that difficulty, I'm sure. What I wonder about is whether we shall be able to get permission to dig here."

"Shall we have to ask leave?" cried Tom, in great surprise.

"It is n't our land, is it?" answered his uncle.

"But it is our money," Tom urged in response.

Mr. Rapallo smiled. "The money is yours, no doubt," he said; "but it will be best for you to get the right to see if it is buried here."

"And suppose we can't get it?" Tom demanded.

"We'll discuss that when the permission is refused. Don't cross the stream till you get there. In the mean time I'll look up the owner of this land—"

"But I don't know who owns it," said Tom.

"I can find out all about it, down-town to-morrow; and that's the first thing to do. It is our duty at least to try to get permission to enter on another man's land. As you grow older, Tom, you will find that the short cut is the straight way."

That evening, when they were finishing their supper, there

came a sudden clang of bells and the rattling rush of a fire-engine.

"There's a fire!" cried Tom, with an appealing look at his mother. Tom had the American boy's intense fondness for going to see fires; but his mother did not like to have him run after the engine at night, as many other lads were allowed to do.

"I pity the poor people whose house it is!" said Mrs. Paulding, not replying to Tom's glance of appeal.

"It's a long while since I have seen a fire here," Uncle Dick remarked, rising from the table. "I think I shall go and take a look at it. Would you like to come, too, Tom?"

"Wouldn't I just?" Tom replied, as the hose-carriage rattled past the house in hot pursuit of its engine. "May I go, mother?"

"Let him come with me," said Uncle Dick. "I'll keep guard over him, and I'll return him right side up with care."

"Wrap yourself up well, Tom," said his mother.

"I wish I was a boy and could go to fires," declared Pauline. "When I'm grown up I shall live next door to an engine-house, and I'll make friends with the firemen, and when there's a great, big fire, I'll get them to let me ride on the engine."

As Uncle Dick and Tom were leaving the house, Mr. Rapallo turned back and said to his sister:

"Mary, don't be uneasy about this boy, and don't sit up for him. If there's anything to see, I shall not hurry back, and Tom will stay with me."

It was lucky that Mrs. Paulding had thus been warned, as her brother and her son returned to the house long after midnight.

By the fiery track of the glowing sparks which the engine

UNCLE DICK AND TOM GO TO THE FIRE.

had left behind it, Mr. Rapallo and Tom were able to go direct to the conflagration, one of the largest ever seen on that part of Manhattan Island. The fire had begun, no one knew how, in a new warehouse, which had recently been completed at the water's edge, between the railroad and a narrow wharf built out into the river. This building, half filled with combustible goods, was blazing fiercely when Uncle Dick and Tom came out at the upper end of the Riverside Drive, where they could look down into the fiery furnace on the bank of the frozen river below.

Tom found Cissy Smith standing there with his father; and while Dr. Smith and Mr. Rapallo renewed their acquaintance, broken off since Uncle Dick had last been in Denver, five years before, Cissy greeted Tom heartily.

"That's a bully old fire, is n't it?" he cried.

"It's the biggest I've ever seen," Tom responded.

From the first the firemen seemed hopeless of saving the warehouse where the fire had started, for the flames had gained full control over it before a single engine was able to throw a stream on it. There was difficulty in getting water, as more than one hydrant was frozen solid; it took precious time to thaw them out by building bonfires all over them. The center of the river was still open and the ice inshore was not so thick that a resolute steamboat could not crush through it. Soon after Tom and Cissy had taken their places to see the spectacle, a fire-boat came up the river and forced its way through the ice till it stopped almost alongside the burning building. Leaving this boat to attend to the warehouse, the firemen ashore turned their attention chiefly to preventing the spread of the conflagration. There was a lumber-yard, piled high with boards and planks, within a hundred feet of the blazing storehouse, and the saving of this was a work of great difficulty. The labor of the firemen was made doubly severe by a chill wind which blew up the river, carrying the flames toward the tall piles of planks, scattering sparks over the neighboring houses, and freezing the water almost as it left the nozles of the hose. Despite the intense heat of the burning building, long icicles began to descend from every projecting plank in the yard, and the firemen were soon clad in a frozen coat of mail, stiff and crackling as the wearers went about their work.

While the two boys were standing there on the hilltop, enjoying the magnificent spectacle, with no thought of the cost at which it was provided, and accepting it as a sort of unexpected and superior Fourth-of-July celebration, Corkscrew Lott came twisting up the hill toward them, as fast as his high boots would carry him. As he drew near it seemed to Tom that Lott was taller than ever.

"He's getting on for six feet," said Tom, involuntarily.

"'Ill weeds grow apace,'" returned Cissy; "at least that's what my father says."

"I say, Cissy," cried Lott, approaching hastily, "where's your father?"

"He's here," Cissy answered. "What's the matter?"

"They want the doctor quick, down at little Jimmy Wigger's aunt's," Lott replied.

"Who's hurt?" Tom asked.

"It's little Jimmy himself," Lott responded. "His aunt sent him out on an errand, and he did n't look sharp, and one of the engines came around a corner and ran over him, and they think he's broken something inside."

Cissy told his father, and under Corkscrew's guidance Dr. Smith and his son went off to the house of little Jimmy's aunt.

Tom and Uncle Dick stood watching the fire that was leaping higher than ever, in despite of the long curves of water which spent themselves in vain in their attack on it. The steam from the engines rose white in the night air, and the ruddy glare of the fire colored the arching lines of water that the steamboat poured into the burning building.

"There's a sort of likeness in this operation," said Uncle Dick, "to hydraulic mining. At Monotony Dam, in California, I have seen a bigger stream than all those put together; and, when the full head of water was turned on, it would eat into the side of a hill and wash out the pay-gravel by the ton."

Tom, being greatly interested by this remark, was about to ask for an explanation of the methods of hydraulic mining, when his uncle turned to him suddenly.

"Tom," he said, hastily, "come to think of it, that's the way you may get at that buried treasure of yours."

"How?" asked Tom.

"We'll turn on a stream of water and wash the guineas out of that bank of rubbish. I've done a good many odd things in my life, first and last, but I confess it will be a novel experience to try hydraulic mining for gold right here in the streets of New York!"

CHAPTER XIV.

THE BATTLE OF THE CURLS.

R. RAPALLO and Tom were so interested in the fire that they were very late in getting to bed. For the first time in his life Tom "heard the chimes at midnight," or at least he heard the bell in the tower of a church near by strike twelve. It was a clear winter night; there was not a cloud in the heavens, but there was no moon, and the sky was dark as if the freezing wind had blown out the stars, which twinkled, chill and remote. In this murk midnight, black and cold, the mighty bonfire by the water's edge blazed away, rolling dense masses of smoke up the river and affording a delightful spectacle to those who were unthinking enough to forget its cost.

It was after one o'clock when Uncle Dick and Tom returned home. Everybody had gone to bed hours before; but Mrs. Paulding's quick ear recognized her boy's footstep on the stairs as he went up to his room.

Five minutes after he entered the house he was in bed and asleep. Indeed, it seemed as if he was in his first nap when there came a rap on the door, and Katie's voice was heard.

"Get up out o' that bed, Master Tom. Sure it's gettin' cold the breakfast is, an' it's the buckwheat cakes ye like that ye 're missin'. Mr. Richard has been 'atin' away this last half hour."

Thus aroused and besought, Tom got out of bed and dressed sleepily. Even when he took his seat at the breakfast-table he was not yet wide awake.

To his great surprise Uncle Dick looked as fresh as if he had had ten hours' rest.

"Oh, Tom," cried Polly, "you are very late!"

"Better late than never," Tom replied, cheerfully but drowsily, as he helped himself to the buckwheat cakes.

"You've got sleep in your eyes still," said Uncle Dick.

"I shall be all right in a minute," Tom declared. "I suppose it is the light that makes my eyes blink."

"I don't know how you would manage if you were on a long march," Uncle Dick went on, "when you had to walk twenty hours out of twenty-four for three or four days together."

"I could n't manage it at all," Tom confessed; "that is, not without training for it. I suppose that one can train for anything, even for going without sleep."

Mr. Rapallo laughed. "I should n't like to make trial of that. I think the result would be not unlike the experience of the man who believed that eating was all a matter of habit, and that a horse could be gradually accustomed to live on nothing. Unfortunately for the success of the experiment, just when he was getting the horse trained down — it died."

"Oh," said Polly, "I don't see how people can ever be so cruel to horses or dogs or cats. It's hateful."

"Experiments are rarely pleasant for those on whom they are tried," Uncle Dick returned. "They are like practical jokes, in that respect."

When Tom had finished his breakfast, his mother left the dining-room for a conference with the Brilliant Conversationalist. Her son stood for a moment before the fireplace.

"I think that you had better go upstairs again and take another nap," suggested his uncle, noticing how the boy's eyes were closing involuntarily.

"I'm not very sleepy," Tom asserted, rousing himself with an effort. "Besides, I could n't go to sleep if I wanted to. Cissy Smith and a lot more boys are going coasting this morning. Cissy is coming for me."

There was a lounge on one side of the dining-room. Tom walked over to it with affected unconcern.

"I've nothing to do to-day," he exclaimed, "and I think I'll just lie down here and shut my eyes till the boys come."

Pauline slipped off her uncle's knees and drew a shawl over Tom as he lay on the lounge.

"Marmee says," she remarked, sagely, as she did this, "that you must never go to sleep without something over you."

"But I'm not going to sleep," Tom declared.

The little girl pulled the shawl up to his shoulders and tucked it in. Then she stood for a moment at the head of the lounge, smoothing her brother's hair.

"I wish I had curls like yours, Tom," she said; "they

would be so becoming on a girl, and they are just wasted on you."

"Pauline," her uncle called to her, gently, "better leave your brother alone and let him have his nap."

"I don't want a nap," asserted Tom, as he turned over; and in less than sixty seconds the regularity of his breathing was very like a snore.

Uncle Dick laughed gently. "The boy was up late last night. No wonder he can't keep awake."

He parted with Polly at the door.

"Good-by, Polly," he said, "I'm going down-town — to work."

"Have n't you any Christmas holidays?" she asked, sympathetically.

"No," her uncle answered. "The Christmas vacation is intended only for boys and girls, because they have had to labor hard over their lessons all the fall. Of course grown-up men don't work so much, and therefore they don't need it."

"Then I'm glad I'm not going to be a grown-up man," returned Pauline.

After her uncle had gone she patted Tom's curls, trying to smooth them and then disarranging them completely — without in any way disturbing his sound slumber.

"How they do curl!" she thought. "I wonder if I could make them curl the other way."

So she got half a dozen little pieces of paper and began to twist her brother's locks up in them. He still slept on. She was careful not to pull the distorted curls. In a few minutes Tom's head was covered with half a dozen little twists of paper.

"I do wonder, really," she said to herself, "whether that will take any of his curls out of curl, or whether it will make them curl the other way. It will be most curious to see."

She moved across the room to judge of the possible effect; and then her mother called to her and she flitted lightly upstairs, leaving her brother fast asleep, all unconscious of the adornment of his head with little twisted bits of paper.

Tom lay there for nearly an hour, and then he was awakened by the signal of the Black Band outside the window.

It was not until Cissy Smith had whistled twice that Tom was aroused sufficiently to understand that his friend had come for him.

He sprang from the lounge and rushed into the hall. He put on his cap and, while he was getting his overcoat buttoned, he opened the door and returned the signal.

"Is that your new sled?" he cried, as he came out and found Cissy Smith waiting for him. "It's a beauty!"

"It's my best Christmas present," Cissy declared. "Father had it made for me at the same place one was made for him when he was a boy. You can't buy them anywhere; you have to order them a year ahead."

The sled was worthy of praise. It was a shapely and seemly piece of work. It stood high from the ground on two firm but delicate runners, shod and braced with steel. Its slender length was not disfigured by paint, but the tough wood showed clear-grained through the white varnish.

After the sled had been duly admired, Tom and Cissy set out for the hillside where they were to coast.

At the first corner, they met Lott and Harry Zachary; and other boys joined them as they went on.

Lott asked Cissy, "How is little Jimmy Wigger this morning?" and he twisted himself into an interrogation-mark in his anxiety to get all the details of the sad story.

Cissy reported that the little boy was not improving.

"If his back is hurt," suggested Harry Zachary, gently, "I reckon the doctors will have to cut out his backbone, maybe, or amputate both his legs."

"Pop says that little Jimmy is going to have a close call," Cissy Smith declared, conscious of the advantage he had in being the doctor's son.

"A call, eh?" Harry Zachary returned. "Well, I reckon he's right. We ought to go over and see how he is this morning."

"Pop says he is n't any better," Cissy Smith asserted.

"We're not calling to find out how he is, but just out of manners," explained Harry.

"Then come along," replied Cissy, lurching ahead in his usual rolling gait.

"And when they tell him we've been there," Tom interjected, "perhaps it will make him feel better."

"Do you suppose that they will really cut off his legs?" asked Lott.

"Corkscrew would n't like to have his legs cut off," Tom remarked, at large, "because he 'keeps his brains in his boots.'"

The boys greeted with a hearty laugh this allusion to a recent remark of one of the school-teachers about Lott—a remark which was nearer the truth than the teacher suspected.

Lott's insatiate curiosity did not extend to his lessons at school. In these he took no interest whatever. He rarely studied. In his recitations he relied on the help of the boys who might be next to him and on even less lawful aids. He had picked up a key to the arithmetic used in the school; and this illegal assistant to recitation he used to take into class with him every day; at least, he took with him the one or two pages containing the answers needed in the lesson of the day. These loose leaves he concealed in a secret place feasible only to himself,— for no one else wore such tall boots. The tops of these boots projected above his knees when he sat down; and behind the shields thus erected Corkscrew placed the needed pages of the key. The room in which arithmetic was taught was overcrowded; and Corkscrew's recent sudden growth, and his strange habit of twisting about, and his enormous boots, all made him conspicuous. It was as if he was taking up more than his share of the room. The teacher especially disliked the boots, and various remarks were directed against them. The last of these remarks was to the effect that "there is no use saying anything more about Lott's boots; he will not part with them; I believe he keeps his brains in those boots."

When Tom Paulding recalled this remark of the teacher's, Lott did not like it. But he could think of no other retort than to say, "You are ever so smart, you are!"

As Tom failed to reply to this taunt, it seemed less effective than Corkscrew could have desired.

The boys had now come to the brow of the hill down which they were to coast.

In default of any more cutting response to the remark about the boots, Lott seized Tom's cap and threw it as far as he could down the hillside.

If Tom Paulding had not made Corkscrew angry by an unprovoked allusion, he would not have exposed himself to this sudden exhibition of his own head with its adornment of little twists of paper—all unknown to Tom himself.

"Who curled your hair?" asked Cissy, when the cap was plucked from Tom's head.

"What do you mean?" cried Tom, partly to Lott and partly to Cissy.

By this time Lott, who had been watching the cap as it circled through the air and then slid along the glassy surface of the slide, had caught sight of the half-dozen bits of paper which bedecked Tom's head.

"Ah, ha!" he cried, "I told you Tom put his hair up in paper!"

"I don't," said Tom.

"Don't you?" shouted Lott, forcibly. "You tell that to a blind man. We can see for ourselves."

"I never curled my hair in my life!" Tom declared.

"Then who put it up in paper for you this morning, Tom?" was Corkscrew's triumphant question.

Involuntarily Tom raised his hand to his head, and he felt the little twists of paper. The boys laughed,—even Cissy Smith, Tom's best friend, and not an admirer of Lott's, joined in the merriment. Tom felt his face burning red as he pulled out the papers.

Then he turned to Lott.

"Go get my cap," he said, angrily.

"I won't," answered Lott. "If you had n't said anything about my boots, I should n't have touched your cap. And I 'm glad I did now, for I 've shown everybody how you get your pretty curls."

"Will you get that cap?" repeated Tom.

"No, I won't," Lott replied.

"Then I 'll make you," said Tom.

"I 'd like to see you do it," was Lott's retort—although this was exactly what he would not like to see.

There is no need to describe a boys' quarrel after it ends in an appeal to arms—and fists. The battle between Tom Paulding and Corkscrew Lott began promptly, and, for a while, its issue was in doubt. Lott was older than Tom, and taller and heavier; but, of late, he had been growing beyond his strength. In the end, Tom had the best of it. But Corkscrew did not go after Tom's cap. This gage of battle had been brought back by one of the smaller boys during a pause in the fight. So it happened that Tom's was but a barren

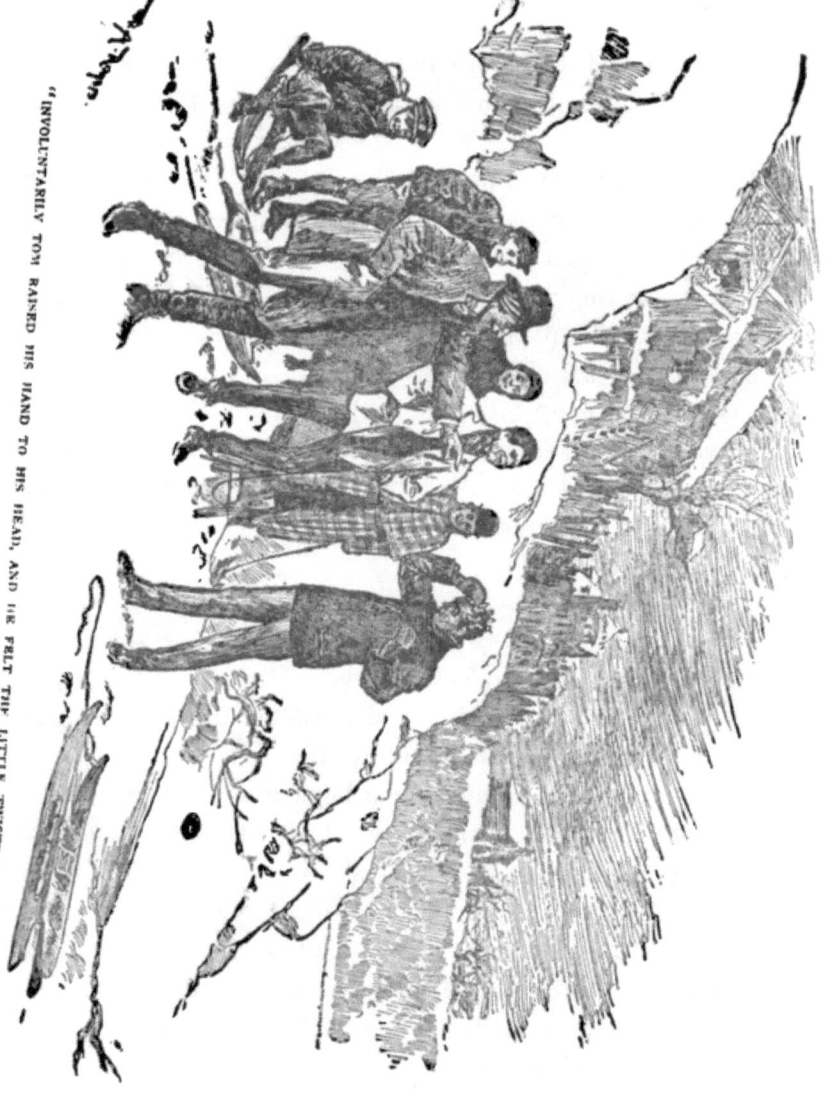

"INVOLUNTARILY TOM RAISED HIS HAND TO HIS HEAD, AND HE FELT THE LITTLE TWISTS OF PAPER."

victory—like nearly all those a boy gains except when he conquers himself.

Lott and several friends of his went away to coast down another hill. Tom, when he had recovered his wind and stanched his wounds, joined in the sport with Cissy and Harry Zachary. But when he left the slide and went home to his dinner, he bore with him the scars of war in the shape of a swollen face and an unmistakable black eye.

CHAPTER XV.

A NEW-YEAR'S-DAY DEPARTURE.

TOM did not quite know what to do about his black eye. He knew that his mother would see it, and then she would be sure to ask him about it, and he would have to tell her the whole story. That she would not approve of the fight Tom felt sure; and he was a little in doubt whether he himself quite approved of it. He had often thought that sooner or later he and Corkscrew would have to "have it out"; and if the combat had been really inevitable, he was glad that it was over and that he had not come out of it second-best. But even in the glow of victory, he did not feel altogether satisfied with the way in which war had been declared nor with his own conduct in the beginning. His reference to Lott's keeping his brains in his boots was altogether uncalled for. It is true that Corkscrew's throwing of the cap down-hill had slight justification. But, all the same, Tom had an uneasy consciousness that the real cause of the anger that had burned so fiercely in his breast was in great measure the keen mortification arising from

the disclosure of his hair curled up in paper. And Tom knew that it was Polly who had bedecked his head with twists of paper, and not Corkscrew. Still they would never have been seen had it not been for Corkscrew. And so, after all—

Tom had gone thus far in the examination of his conscience when he reached home.

As the Careful Katie opened the door, she caught sight of the black eye.

"Oh, Master Tom!" she cried, "is it in a fight ye 've been?"

"Yes," Tom answered. "I 've been in a fight."

"Come into the kitchen, then," she went on, heartily, "and I 'll give ye a bit of beefsteak to put on yer eye. An' ye can tell me all about the fight the while. Sure, beefsteak is the wan thing for a black eye. It 's many a time me brothers would have liked a bit, a-comin' back from a fair in Killaloo, or a wake, or any other merrymakin'."

Tom was following the Brilliant Conversationalist into the kitchen, when Pauline came dancing out into the hall.

"Oh, Tom," she cried, "what do you think? We 've three new kittens, one black, and one white with a black eye, and one all gray—ever so pretty. And Marmee says I may keep the gray one, and I 'm going to. The one that 's white with the black eye is smaller and cunninger, but I don't like a white kitten with a black eye, do you? It looks just as if it had been fighting, and of course it has n't yet, for it 's only two hours old."

Tom smiled grimly. "I 'd keep the one with the black

eye," he said, as he followed Katie into the kitchen, "and you might call it after me." And with that he turned his head so that she could see his face.

"Oh, Tom!" Polly exclaimed. "You look worse than the kitten — ever so much worse!"

"Perhaps," said Tom, dolefully, "when the kitten gets a little older, you will put its tail up in curl-papers; and then it will go out, and come back again with a black eye bigger than mine."

"It would be cruel to twist up a cat's tail!" she declared.

"Was n't it cruel to let me go out with my hair in curl-papers?" he rejoined.

"Did you?" she cried, penitently. "Oh, Tom, I 'm so sorry! I did n't mean to. I never thought. I 'll never do it again; I 'll be so good next time. I don't see how I ever came to do it. Won't you forgive me this time?"

Tom made haste to forgive her when he saw how sorrowful she looked.

Then the Brilliant Conversationalist came with a bit of raw beef and placed this to the injured eye and tied it tight with Tom's handkerchief bound about his head.

"There," she said, "that 'll draw out the poison for you. Now tell us about the fight. Did ye bate the head off the villain?"

Then Tom, half pleased and half ashamed, told his sister and Katie all about the combat with Corkscrew Lott.

"Oh, Tom!" Pauline cried suddenly, "what will Marmee say?"

A NEW-YEAR'S-DAY DEPARTURE.

"I don't know," replied Tom, doubtfully. "She won't like it."

"Shall I go and break the news to her gently, as they do in the story-books?" suggested his sister.

"No," Tom answered; "I'd better tell her myself."

"I'll go with you," Pauline persisted; "and I'll tell her it was all my fault."

"No," Tom replied again, "I'd better go alone."

So he took heart of grace, and went up to his mother's room and placed before her the whole story; not trying to shield himself, but as well as he could telling the truth, the whole truth, and nothing but the truth.

Mrs. Paulding was a wise mother. She saw that her son had been punished; she did not reproach him, but she spoke to him gently, and when she had ceased speaking Tom had made up his mind never to get into another fight. Then she kissed him, and they went down together to their early dinner.

That evening, when Uncle Dick returned, the whole story had to be gone over once more. It is to be recorded with regret that Mr. Rapallo laughed heartily when he heard about the curls which Polly put up in paper and which Corkscrew revealed accidentally.

"Best keep out of a fight if you can," he said when he had heard the full details; "but if you must fight, go in to win."

"I don't think I shall go in again," Tom declared, looking up at his mother with an affectionate glance, which would have been more effective if the black eye had not been still covered by the bit of beefsteak and the handkerchief.

"Sure if he goes to a wake, any dacent boy may have to swing his shillalah about a bit," the Careful Katie remarked, as she left the room for the preserves.

"The Brilliant Conversationalist is in favor of a free fight," Uncle Dick declared. "But I'll give you a Spanish proverb better than her Hibernian advice — and there is no more honorable race than the Spanish, and no one is more punctilious than a Spaniard. Yet they have a saying, 'It is the man who returns the first blow who begins the quarrel.'"

After supper, Mrs. Paulding and Pauline went upstairs, leaving Mr. Rapallo and Tom alone together.

"I've been looking up the ownership of that property where you think your guineas are," said Uncle Dick.

"Did you find out?" Tom asked, eagerly.

"I found that the land is in dispute," his uncle replied. "The title to it is doubtful, and there has been a lawsuit about it in the courts now for nearly ten years."

"But it must belong to some one," Tom insisted.

"It's likely to belong to the lawyers, if this litigation does n't stop soon," Uncle Dick answered. Then he explained how it was:

"The case seems to be complicated; there was an assignment of some sort made by the original owner fifty years ago; and now there are two mortgages and two wills, and half a dozen codicils. And all the parties are angry, and there is 'blood on the moon.' So I'm afraid that when we get ready to dig for that buried treasure, we shall have to do it without asking anybody's permission. In the first place, we don't know whom to ask; and in the second place, whoever we ask would surely suspect us of coming from one of the other parties, and would not only refuse but perhaps set a guard on the property or have detectives watch us."

"Oh!" said Tom, and he was conscious of a certain swelling pride at the possibility that there might be a detective "on his track," as he phrased it.

"Of course," Mr. Rapallo continued, "as long as the frost's in the ground there is no use in our trying to do anything. In the meanwhile, you will say nothing."

"Not even to Cissy Smith?" Tom urged, aware of the delight that he would have in imparting this real mystery to his friend.

"Not even to anybody," Uncle Dick answered. "If Cissy were to tell some one, you could n't blame him for not keeping the secret you could n't keep yourself."

Tom felt the force of this reasoning, but he regretted that his uncle thought it best not to tell Cissy. Tom felt sure of Cissy's discretion, and he longed to have some one with whom to talk over the buried treasure. Thus early in life Tom was made to see the wisdom in the saying of the philosopher, that a secret is a most undesirable property, for "if you tell it, you have n't got it; and if you don't tell it, you lose the interest on the investment."

The next afternoon, as Tom was coming back from asking how little Jimmy Wigger was getting on, he saw Mr. Rapallo standing on the stoop of Mr. Joshua Hoffmann's house talking to the old gentleman he had before seen leaning over the wall. Tom supposed that the Old Gentleman who leaned over the Wall, as he called him in his own mind, was probably Mr. Hoffmann himself, but he was not quite sure of it.

Once again before New Year's Day, Tom saw his uncle in conference with the Old Gentleman who leaned over the Wall. Tom noticed that about this time Mr. Rapallo was a little more restless than usual; and then again that he would sink into frequent fits of thoughtful silence.

On New Year's morning, Mr. Rapallo caught Tom's eye, after Tom had spoken twice without bringing him out of his silent abstraction.

"I beg your pardon, Tom," he said; "I was thinking. The fact is, I've got the idea of a little invention buzzing in my head, and I keep turning it over and over, and looking at it on all sides, even when I ought to be doing something else — eating my breakfast, for example."

They were then at their morning meal; and just at that moment the shrill whistle of the postman was heard.

"There does be only one letter-man this mornin', I'm thinkin'," said the Brilliant Conversationalist, as she went out to see what the postman had for them.

"There may be a letter for me," Uncle Dick remarked, "that will take me away to-night."

"You are not going to leave us?" cried Polly.

"I may have to go," her uncle answered.

"Where?" she asked.

A NEW-YEAR'S-DAY DEPARTURE.

"On a journey—to lots of places," he replied.

"How long will you be gone?" she went on.

"I don't know. Two or three months, perhaps," he answered. Then, catching Tom's inquiring glance, he added, "I shall be back by the time the frost is out of the ground. I'm like a bad penny, I'm sure to turn up again."

"You are not a bad penny at all," said Polly, with emphasis. "You are as good as gold, and a penny is only copper. And if you have to go, we shall all miss you very, very much!" Then she got up and walked around the table and kissed her uncle on the cheek.

Katie returned and gave Uncle Dick the only letter she had in her hand.

"The letter-man says he does n't be comin' here again to-day, mum, but ye can give him his New Year's in the mornin'," she reported.

"Must you go?" asked Mrs. Paulding, who had watched her brother's face as he read the note.

"Yes. I must start this afternoon at the latest," he answered. "It is to see a man about this little invention of mine. If he likes it, we shall work it out together. Then, when I come back in the spring, Mary, I hope to bring you that Christmas present I owe you."

When Mr. Rapallo left the house, about twelve o'clock, Tom went with him to the nearest elevated-railroad station. Uncle Dick did not walk this time, as he had a heavy bag to carry.

After Mr. Rapallo and Tom had stepped down upon the sidewalk, from the flight of wooden steps leading from the street up to the rocky crest on which the house was perched, they saw Cissy Smith. He was coming eagerly toward them.

"Have you heard the news about little Jimmy?" asked Cissy.

"No," Tom replied. "What is it?"

"He died this morning early," Cissy continued. "Father was there. Little Jimmy did not suffer any. And he could n't ever have been strong again."

"Poor little chap!" said Tom, thinking of the eagerness of the little fellow as he had followed Tom about ready to do his bidding, whatever it might be.

"The years bring joy to some and sorrow to others," Mr. Rapallo remarked gently; "but it is a sad house to which Death pays a New Year's call."

CHAPTER XVI.

TOM HAS PATIENCE.

TWO days after New Year's, little Jimmy Wigger was buried, and all the boys of the Black Band attended the funeral. Eight of them, including Tom Paulding, Cissy Smith, G. W. Lott, and Harry Zachary, were asked to be pall-bearers. Tom long remembered his silent walk by the side of the coffin as one of the saddest duties he had ever performed.

The next Monday school began again, and Tom went back to work. Now that he believed he knew where the stolen guineas were, and now that he expected to recover them with his uncle's assistance, his hope of being able to go to the School of Mines increased, and he studied harder than ever before that he might fit himself as soon as possible for this new undertaking. Unless something happened to help Mrs. Paulding, Tom knew that at the end of the year he would have to give up his aspirations and take a place in a store, that his earnings might contribute to the support of the family. If he could find the buried treasure, he felt sure that the money would suffice to tide over the difficulties of the household until after he had been through the School of Mines, and was able to make his living as a man, and to support his mother and sister on his income as an engineer. During the Christmas vacation, after his uncle had gone, Tom had walked down to Columbia College and had found out the requirements for admission. He believed that he could pass the examination the next year, late in the spring, if he could keep on with his studies until then. And whether he could do this or not depended now absolutely on the finding of the two thousand guineas stolen from his great-grandfather.

At the house, they all missed Uncle Dick. In the two months that Mr. Rapallo had spent at Mrs. Paulding's he had made himself quite at home, and they had come to look on him as a permanent member of the family. Mrs. Paulding had greatly enjoyed the long quiet talks she had had with her brother after her children were gone to bed. Pauline missed a playfellow always ready to join in her sports and always quick to devise a fresh game. Even the Brilliant Conversationalist grieved over Mr. Rapallo's departure. Certain little dishes of which he had been especially fond she ceased to serve, explaining that she would make these again "after Mr. Richard do be back."

But Tom missed him most of all. He felt lonely without Uncle Dick, who was older than he by nearly thirty years, yet who was always able to look at things from his point of view. The man and the boy had been very companionable, one to the other. Until long afterward, Tom did not know how much his character had been influenced by the example of his Uncle Dick, and how much Mr. Rapallo's shrewd and pithy talks had affected his views of life.

What Tom most needed was some one with whom he could discuss the buried treasure. He was young, and youth is sanguine; and he felt sure that the stolen guineas were really where he thought they were. But he wanted to have some one to whom he could talk about them, so as to keep up his own enthusiasm. There were days, during the absence of Uncle Dick, when it was very difficult for Tom not to tell Cissy Smith, despite Mr. Rapallo's warning. The secret burned within him and sometimes it almost burst forth of its own accord. Tom was strong enough to resist the temptation. He did not like to have to confess to his uncle that he had disregarded the warning. Besides, he was a little in doubt how Cissy would accept the revelation; Cissy was a skeptical boy, with a superabundance of cold common sense. In imagination, when Tom told Cissy all about the buried treasure, and when he came to the long string of mere probabilities on which its discovery depended, he shivered as he fancied that he heard Cissy's frank opinion:

"Shucks! I don't take any stock in fairy-stories like that."

So Tom told no one. Yet the effort to bottle up his great secret must have been obvious at times. Corkscrew Lott became aware of it, or at least suspicious that something was on Tom's mind. Corkscrew's curiosity was greater than his pride, and he made up with Tom before they had been back at school for a week. He threw himself in Tom's way whenever Tom went out for a walk. In some strange manner he discovered that Tom was interested in the vacant lot where the stepping-stones were; and once, when Tom was drawn — as he often was — to go and look at the bank of earth beneath which he believed his treasure lay hidden, he found Corkscrew prowling around in the lot, and poking into its corners as if to spy out Tom's secret.

Corkscrew's curiosity went so far that he even stopped Pauline one day, as she was going home from school, to ask a few questions about Tom's doings, vainly endeavoring to entrap her into some admission as to the cause of her brother's change of manner.

"I did n't know he had changed at all," Polly answered, simply.

"Oh, I did n't know, either," explained Corkscrew. "I only thought that, maybe, you know, he might have got on the track of that buried treasure, or stolen money, or something of that sort, that used to belong to his great-great-great-grandfather, once upon a time."

When this was repeated to Tom, he regretted that he had ever mentioned the loss of the two thousand guineas to any of the Black Band, and most of all that he had said anything in Corkscrew's hearing. He resolved to keep away from the stepping-stones until Uncle Dick returned.

Then it struck him that it would be fun to lead Corkscrew off on a false scent. So whenever he had part of an afternoon to spare, he would start off to Morningside Park, and as

TOM HAS PATIENCE. 175

he took care to let Lott know where he was going, he soon had the satisfaction of seeing Corkscrew skulking along a block or so behind him. Tom would go gravely down the stone steps of Morningside Park, and he would pretend to

"TOM WOULD PRETEND TO SOUND ROCKS WITH A STICK."

sound rocks with a stick and to peer into all the crevices he could find. Sometimes he would push on down to Central Park when he was sure that Corkscrew was following; and then he would go all over the old fort which is still standing at the upper end of the park.

And so the winter passed. Early in January there was a gentle thaw; and Tom hoped that the cold weather was over and that the ground would soon be soft enough for them to begin to dig. But on the day before Washington's Birthday there came a terrific snow-storm, covering the earth with a white mantle nearly a yard thick. The wind blew fiercely down the Hudson, tossing the snow-wreaths high in the air, and swirling them off down the hillside into the river. Then there followed a hard frost, and the thermometer fell day after day, and the wind blew keener and keener.

All things come to an end in time, and the winter was over before Tom or his mother had any word from Richard Rapallo.

"Don't expect to hear from me till you see me," he had said to his sister just before he left the house. "You know I'm not 'The Complete Letter-Writer.' If I get my work done, I'll drop in again when you least expect me."

As the season advanced, and after the final thaw had come, the boys gave up coasting and skating, and began kite-flying. The river was open again, although huge fields of ice still came floating past. There were signs of spring at last. Across the river, up near the Palisades, there began to be a hint of fresh verdure. The long tows were once more to be seen moving slowly up and down the river.

The trees on the hillside below the Riverside Drive and the few bushes about Mrs. Paulding's house were green again before there was any news of Uncle Dick. The hard part— or at least so Tom thought it—was that they did not know where Mr. Rapallo was. Sometimes Tom saw the Old Gentleman who leaned over the Wall walking slowly along the parapet of the drive before his house, as if he were inhaling the freshness of the spring; and Tom wondered if this benevolent-looking old gentleman knew where Uncle Dick was, and whether he would be greatly offended if Tom should go up and ask him.

One day when spring was well advanced,—it was then about the middle of April,—Tom determined to walk past the vacant lots where the stepping-stones were, that he might at least enjoy the sight of the outward covering of the wealth he was seeking. To his dismay he found that there was a cart standing on the tongue of land projecting out to the stepping-stones, and that this cart was but one of a dozen or more engaged in emptying builder's rubbish.

Tom did not know what to do. If these lots were to be filled up, then the difficulty of recovering the buried treasure would be doubled. Of course he saw that he could oppose no resistance to the work; he had to suffer in silence.

The next day, when he went to see how far the filling had progressed, he was delighted to find that the rubbish was now being emptied at one of the upper corners of the block, and that the fence had been replaced across the tongue of land which led out to the stepping-stones.

About that time there came a week of warm weather, and it seemed indisputable that there would be no more frost till the fall. Still there was no word from Uncle Dick. Tom thought that the hour had come when an effort ought to be made to get at the buried treasure; but he himself did not know how to go to work. He had relied on his uncle's help.

Suddenly the fear came to him that perhaps Uncle Dick would not return to them until too late. What would Tom do then?

As the days drew on, Tom became more and more doubtful about his uncle's coming. At last he determined to wait no longer, but to see what he could do by himself.

He recalled what Mr. Rapallo had said about hydraulic mining on the night of the fire, when little Jimmy was run over. Uncle Dick had declared that the stolen guineas could best be got at by hydraulic mining. What that was Tom did not know. He resolved to find out.

One Saturday afternoon he went down to the Apprentices' Library, and took out a book which the kindly librarian indicated as likely to give him the best account of the process. The next Saturday he got another volume; and a third Saturday he spent in looking up articles in the cyclopedias and in the bound magazines where the librarian had told him to search. From these, some of which were fully illustrated, Tom managed to get an understanding of the principles of hydraulic mining; and he thought he saw how his uncle meant to apply them to the getting out of the two thousand guineas buried near the stepping-stones.

Hydraulic mining is the name given in the West to the method of washing out a hillside containing auriferous sands by the impact of a stream of water, which carries down, into a prepared channel in the valley below, the "pay gravel" in the hill on both sides. After Tom had mastered the suggestion, he saw that his uncle meant in like manner to wash away the dirt and sand which hid the remains of Jeffrey Kerr.

The stepping-stones were near the upper end of the vacant block, and the ground sloped sharply away below, where the brook had run formerly. Tom saw that if a little channel were dug around two projecting rocks, it would then be easy to wash out the loose earth, partly rubbish and partly sand, which formed the projecting point over the stepping-stones. If his guess as to the present position of the stolen money were right, then he would have to wear into the bank a hole fully twenty feet deep. With the aid of the small canal Tom had planned, he thought he saw his way clear to a most successful operation in hydraulic mining — if he could only get plenty of water.

Where the water was to come from, was a question for which he had no answer. Uncle Dick had suggested that the buried treasure could be got out by hydraulic mining, but he had not hinted how he was to get the water.

While Tom was puzzling over this to no purpose, one warm sunny day in May, when the leaves were opening on the trees and the bushes, Uncle Dick came back most unexpectedly.

He gave no account of his wanderings; he offered no explanation of his long absence; but from chance allusions in his conversation Tom and Polly made out that he had been traveling part of the time he had been away, and that he had been to Boston, and to Chicago, and possibly even as far as San Francisco.

After supper he asked Tom to come up to his room.

When Tom had followed his uncle out of the dining-room, Polly asked her mother anxiously, "Did Uncle Dick bring you that Christmas present he owes you?"

"He has not given it to me yet," Mrs. Paulding answered; "but he will some day."

"I wish he would," said Pauline. "I do so want to know what it is."

CHAPTER XVII.

ENLISTING ALLIES.

NCLE DICK and Tom had a long conference that evening in the former's room. Tom told his uncle the exact state of affairs. He described how the dumping of rubbish had begun again just over the stepping-stones, and how it had ceased the next day. He set forth Lott's attempt to spy on him, and his own success in throwing Corkscrew's curiosity off the scent. He gave a full account of his own endeavors to discover the methods of hydraulic mining.

"I think I have found out how you mean to go to work, Uncle Dick," he said; "but I confess that I don't see where we are to get the water to wash out all that dirt."

"That will be easy enough," replied his uncle. "We can have all the water we need—when we need it. That will not be for some time yet."

Tom went on to tell Mr. Rapallo how very difficult it had been for him to keep his secret to himself.

"But I have done it!" he concluded. "I have n't said a single, solitary word to anybody."

"I 'm not sure that the time has n't come to take one or two of your friends into your confidence," Uncle Dick responded.

"Can I tell Cissy Smith?" cried Tom; "and Harry Zachary, too?"

"From what you have said to me about your friends," his uncle answered, "I should judge that Cissy and Harry will be your safest allies in this affair."

"Cissy is my best friend," explained the boy, "and Harry is my next-best."

"Do you think they would be willing to help you?" asked Mr. Rapallo.

"Willing?" echoed Tom. "They 'd just be delighted, both of them, to be let into a scheme like this. What do you want them to do?"

"I don't know yet, exactly," his uncle responded; "but there will be work enough of one kind or another. We shall have to dig a trench to carry off the water, for instance."

"They go to school with me, you know, Uncle Dick," said Tom; "and they are free only at the same time that I am,— Saturday afternoons, mostly."

"I think it will be better for you to have a whole day before you—" began Mr. Rapallo.

"Then I don't see how we can come," Tom interrupted, "unless we play hooky."

"Don't you have Decoration Day as a holiday?" asked his uncle.

"Decoration Day?" Tom repeated, with a little disappointment in his voice. "Oh, yes,—but that's more than a fortnight off!"

"I doubt if we shall be ready for a fortnight yet," Mr. Rapallo returned. "There are various things to do before we can turn on the water and wash out the gold—if there's any there to wash out."

"Uncle Dick," cried Tom, piteously, "don't say now that you don't think the gold is there!"

"Oh, yes," Mr. Rapallo answered; "I *think* it is there—but I don't *know*. We have only a 'working hypothesis,' you remember."

"I remember," Tom repeated, dolefully; "but I've been so long thinking about those two thousand guineas lying in the ground there by the stepping-stones that it seems as if I could see them, almost. I feel certain sure they are there!"

"Let us hope so," his uncle responded. "And don't be down-hearted about it. If we are to get that gold, we must all believe that it is there until we know that it is n't."

"I know it *is*," asseverated Tom.

"To-morrow," Mr. Rapallo continued, "you must take your friends into your confidence. I have business downtown and I'll inquire whether the lawyers have found out yet to whom that vacant block belongs. If they have, I'll try to get permission for us to dig out your two thousand guineas."

So the next afternoon, when school was out, Tom Paulding took Cissy Smith and Harry Zachary off with him.

Corkscrew Lott was going to join them, but Tom said to him frankly:

"I've got something particular to say to Cissy and Harry, and so I don't want anybody else to come with us, Lott."

"Can't you tell me, too?" Lott pleaded.

"I can, of course," Tom answered, "if I want to. But I don't."

"Oh, very well!" said Corkscrew, gruffly; "I don't want to know any of your old secrets."

Notwithstanding this disclaimer of all interest in their affairs, Corkscrew lingered at school until after the three other boys had gone on ahead, and then he followed them from afar, in the hope that something unforeseen might reveal the matter of their discourse.

Harry Zachary gave a swift glance back when they came to their first turning. He caught sight of Lott, who stopped short when he saw that he was detected.

"There's Corkscrew on our trail," said Harry. "Let's throw him off the track."

"How are you going to do it?" said Cissy.

"I've got a way," Harry explained. "Follow me."

And with that he turned into the side street, and walked rapidly toward the elevated railroad station.

"Corkscrew will be sure to follow us now," Harry declared; "and when we come to the station, we'll go upstairs. He can't come up after us because he knows we should see him then."

"But we don't want to pay car-fare to nowhere just to get

rid of Corkscrew Lott," remarked Cissy Smith, rolling along a little ahead of the others.

"We need n't pay a cent," Harry Zachary responded. "We can just wait on the outside platform, out of sight from where he is, while we can see him through the window. Then when he goes, we 'll slip down again and run to the Three Trees."

"All right," said Cissy; and Tom also agreed to the plan.

The boys went up the steps of the elevated railroad station; and through the window of the covered platform they saw Corkscrew come up and stare hard at the station and hesitate a little, twisting about as usual. Then he set out to cross the avenue to look at the inner platforms; but, before he could do that, a train from up-town and another from down-town arrived and departed with much puffing and hissing, and shrill squeaking of the brakes. So Corkscrew gave up his effort to "shadow" the three friends, and went on his way home.

As soon as he was gone, Tom, Cissy, and Harry came out of hiding and started off for the Riverside Drive, where there was a favorite spot of theirs, down by the railroad and the river. Here three trees grew in a group, with knotted and distorted branches, so that half a dozen boys could find seats amid their limbs.

When the three friends had arrived at this pleasant place, doubly delightful in the fresh fairness of spring, Tom, who had refused to open the subject before, said solemnly, "Fellows, can you keep a secret?"

"Shucks!" cried Cissy Smith, forcibly. "Did you bring us all the way down here just to tell us a secret? I thought you said you wanted us to help you do something."

"TOM SAID SOLEMNLY, 'FELLOWS, CAN YOU KEEP A SECRET?'"

"Is it about your lost treasure?" asked Harry Zachary, sympathetically.

"How did you know?" Tom inquired, in surprise.

"I don't know; I guessed," Harry explained. "You told us once that you were going to hunt for it, and you've been so different since then that I thought perhaps you had got a notion where it was."

"I have found it!" said Tom, with intense enjoyment of their surprise.

"How much is it?" asked the practical Cissy.

"Where is it?" Harry cried.

"It's two thousand guineas," Tom replied; "and it is now buried far from here. And I want you two to help me get at it."

"Buried?" Cissy repeated. "Then you have not seen it?"

"No," Tom replied, "but I know it's there. It must be there!"

"We'll help you, of course," said Harry Zachary, with a return of his shy and gentle manner. "But we shall have to kill the guards, sha'n't we?"

"What do you mean?" Tom asked, in amazement.

"I suppose there must be somebody guarding this buried treasure, and they must be removed, of course. 'Dead men tell no tales,' you know," Harry explained. "And I have been reading about a new way of getting rid of an enemy; the Italians used to do it in the Middle Ages. You have a glass stiletto,—that's a sort of dagger made of glass,—and you stab the man in the back, and break off the blade, and throw the handle into the Grand Canal; then the man's dead and nobody knows you had anything to do with it."

"I'm glad of that," said Cissy, dryly.

"But is it necessary to kill the guards?" Harry went on. "Would n't it do to give them something to put them to sleep while we get at the treasure? I reckon Cissy could coax his father to give us a prescription for something that would put a whole platoon of police to sleep for the day."

"Shucks!" said Cissy, vigorously. "I'm not going to stab

anybody in the back with a glass dagger, nor are you either, Harry Zachary. And I'm not going to try to put a platoon of police to sleep. It would be what my father calls a 'dangerous experiment.' Suppose some of them did n't wake up, and the rest of them did, and they clubbed the life out of us, where would the fun be then?"

"You need n't quarrel over the glass dagger and the policemen," Tom declared, "because there is n't any guard to kill, this time."

"A buried treasure without any guard?" Harry repeated. "I never heard of such a thing."

"Well," said Tom, "you can hear of it now if you want to listen. But first you have both got to promise that never by thought, word, or deed will you ever reveal any of the secrets I am now about to confide to you."

"That 's all right," Cissy responded, "I won't say a word, —never." Perhaps this delayed double negative served to make the declaration doubly binding.

"I solemnly vow that I will never reveal the secret Thomas Paulding is now about to confide to me," said Harry Zachary, stiffening his usual timid voice. "In China they cut off a chicken's head whenever a man takes an oath before a priest, and that makes it binding, I reckon. I wish we had a chicken here."

"I guess the priests in China are as fond of chicken as anybody else," Cissy commented. "Now, Tom, tell us the whole story."

So Tom began at the beginning, and gave them all the

ENLISTING ALLIES. 189

particulars of his search for the stolen guineas, of the suggestion Santa Claus brought, of the stepping-stones, and of the present situation of the buried treasure.

"That's all very well," said Cissy. "Perhaps the money is there, and perhaps it is n't. How are you to get at it? That's the question."

Then Tom told them about hydraulic mining, explaining briefly to them what he himself had extracted laboriously from many books. He informed them that his uncle was going to arrange for a supply of water, and that Decoration Day had been chosen as the date when the final attack was to be made.

When Tom had finished, Cissy said, "Well, that's a very interesting story, and, as I told you before, maybe the money is there. Leastways, it's worth trying for. I don't see where your uncle is going to get the stream of water—but your uncle is n't any fool, so I guess he knows. And I don't see either where we come in—Harry and I. What are we to do?"

"I don't know just what you will have to do," Tom replied. "But Uncle Dick said to ask you and Harry if you would help us."

"Oh, yes," Cissy responded, heartily. "I'll help all I know how."

After a little further talk the boys started homeward, Cissy lurching along with his usual rolling gait.

"There's the Old Gentleman who leaned over the Wall," said Tom, as they saw a tall, white-haired man get out of a carriage before a handsome house.

"That's Mr. Joshua Hoffmann," explained Harry Zachary. "He's so rich he has more money than he knows what to do with."

"And my father says there is n't a better man in the United States, in spite of all his money," said Cissy.

"My uncle knows him, too," Tom remarked, unwilling to be left out of the conversation.

"Is n't that your uncle now?" asked Harry.

Tom looked across the roadway and saw his uncle stop before the house; and again the old gentleman leaned over the wall to talk to him.

"Yes," said Tom, "that's Uncle Dick."

As the boys went by Mr. Rapallo waved his hand to them; and when Tom glanced back a minute later it seemed as if his uncle were talking about him to the Old Gentleman who leaned over the Wall, for the two men were both looking after the three boys.

The next day, at school, Corkscrew came up to Tom as Cissy and Harry had just joined him.

"Did you three have a nice ride on the railroad, yesterday afternoon?" asked Lott, insidiously.

"I was n't on the cars at all yesterday," said Harry Zachary promptly, with a grave face.

"Neither was I," continued Tom Paulding.

"Nor I," added Cissy Smith.

"I mean the elevated railroad," Corkscrew explained.

"I did n't ride on the elevated railroad yesterday," Harry declared.

"I did n't, either," repeated both Tom and Cissy

"Why, I saw you—" began Lott.

"Oh," said Tom Paulding, "if you know what we've been doing better than we do ourselves, why do you ask questions?"

Corkscrew was a little confused at this. "I happened to be passing the station yesterday," he said, pulling up the tops of his high boots, "and I saw you three go up—"

"If you saw us, then we've nothing to say," Tom interrupted. "But I can tell you that we were none of us in an elevated train yesterday."

"Then why on earth did you—"

But what Corkscrew was going to ask they never knew, as just then the bell rang for school.

CHAPTER XVIII.

MAKING READY.

R. RAPALLO reported to Tom that the title of the vacant block was still in dispute.

"There's no knowing," he said, "when that lawsuit will be settled. It has been going on for seventeen years now, and everybody interested in it has come to hate everybody else; and so they persist in fighting like the 'Kilkenny cats.'"

"Then we can't get permission to look for the two thousand guineas?" Tom asked, anxiously.

"We shall have to do without permission," Uncle Dick replied. "And I suppose that we shall be trespassers when we go into that vacant block to dig up your great-grandfather's gold."

"It is n't our fault that our money is there," said Tom.

"No," his uncle responded. "It is n't our fault, and it is n't the fault of the first owner of the money; whereas if the first owner of the land had exercised proper care over it, he would have refused to harbor on it the body of a thief laden with stolen goods."

"When we find the gold," Tom asked, "do you think the bags in which it was tied will still be there, or will they have rotted away?"

"I should n't wonder if the bags might be gone," Mr. Rapallo replied.

"That's what I thought," Tom continued; "and so I have bought some bagging. It's coarse, but it's very strong — and I don't think we need care about the looks — "

"If the gold looks all right," Uncle Dick interrupted, "I don't think it will matter what we put it in."

"I've asked Polly to make me four bags, just the same number the money was in when my great-grandfather had it," said Tom. "Of course, I didn't tell her what I wanted them for; I don't believe in trusting women with secrets. Do you, Uncle Dick?"

Mr. Rapallo smiled. "As I've told you before," he answered, "the best way to keep your secret safe is to keep it all to yourself. That's one reason I have n't told you yet how I propose to get the water for our hydraulic mining. But come out with me on Saturday afternoon, and I will show you how I mean to manage it."

Since his return from his journey, Mr. Rapallo had settled down into his old way of life at his sister's house. He was still irregular and erratic in his comings and goings. When he went out in the morning, the household never knew when he would return. Some days he seemed to have little or nothing to do, and on other days he was apparently full of engagements. Knowing that Tom was free from his duties only on Saturday afternoon, he arranged to have that time free.

About three o'clock on the Saturday before Decoration Day, he and Tom walked over to the vacant block where the stepping-stones were, for a final examination before they should attempt to find the buried treasure.

The vacant block was of dimensions common enough in New York. It was about two hundred feet wide from street to street, and nearly a thousand feet long from avenue to avenue. The stepping-stones were on the northern side of the block about one third way from the eastern end; and over them projected the tongue of made land which had been filled in mainly with builder's rubbish. The original level of the ground sloped sharply from the east to the west, as the brook had coursed briskly along, hastening away to the Hudson River.

Mr. Rapallo and Tom were pleased to find what they had never noted before, perhaps because the entrance to it was overrun with brambles, that a culvert had been left to carry off the waters of the brook which must, then, have been flowing when the avenue on the western end of the block had been carried across, high in the air above the original level of the land thereabout.

The brook, still easily to be traced by the stunted willows that once lined its bank, had dried up years before Tom and his uncle tramped along its bed; but the culvert survived.

"It is a piece of good fortune," said Mr. Rapallo, "that

the old outlet of the stream is still here. It will serve to take away the water; and now we need not fear that we shall not have fall enough to carry off the waste we shall wash out of the bank."

"But where are you going to get your water?" asked Tom.

"Come and see," his uncle answered, leading the way from the sunken lots to the street-level.

The stepping-stones were perhaps three hundred feet from the northeast corner of the block, and the tongue of land above them projected perhaps fifty or sixty feet into the hollow parallelogram.

Mr. Rapallo took Tom along the sidewalk of the street which bounded the block on the south, until they came opposite the stepping-stones.

"Here," he said, laying his hand on a sort of iron post which rose from the sidewalk at the edge of the gutter, "what is this?"

"That's a hydrant," replied Tom; "that's to supply water to the engines when there's a fire."

"Then why shouldn't it supply us with the water we need?" his uncle asked.

"Well," Tom hesitated a moment. "I suppose it would, perhaps. I don't see why it shouldn't. But how are you going to get a key to turn it on?"

"I've got it already," Mr. Rapallo answered, taking the key from his pocket.

"Oh!" cried Tom. "But how are you going to get

hose to fit this hydrant, and to reach 'way across the block here?"

"I've ordered that," Uncle Dick replied. "I saw that you had done all the thinking over this problem and had worked it out for yourself, so I determined to help you out all I could. I was n't going to see you fail for want of a little aid when you needed it most."

"Uncle Dick, I—" began Tom.

"I know all about it," said his uncle, checking Tom's thanks with a kindly pat on the shoulder. "You need n't say another word."

"But—" the boy began again.

"But me no buts," laughed Mr. Rapallo, "or I will not tell you anything about the hose I have ordered. There will be one section about forty feet long, like fire-engine hose and made to fit this hydrant. Then I shall have perhaps a hundred and twenty-five feet of ordinary garden hose, with a valve and joint so that we can fasten it to the end of the larger hose."

"Won't the difference in size hinder us?" Tom inquired.

"I think not," his uncle answered. "The reduction in the section of the tube through which the water is delivered ought to increase the force of the current as it leaves the nozle—and that is just what we want. The one thing that I am afraid of is that the common or garden hose won't be able to stand the strain put on it. But we shall have to take our chances as to that."

"Is the hose ready?" asked Tom.

"It is to be delivered at the house to-night," Mr. Rapallo replied.

"But then Polly will want to know what it is," Tom suggested promptly.

"And I shall not tell her," Uncle Dick declared; "at least, I shall tell her only that it is something for me."

"Well," Tom continued, "I suppose that she won't dare to ask you too many questions. But she'll be wild to know what it is."

On their way home Tom asked his uncle what time he thought would be the best to begin work on Decoration Day morning.

"The sooner the better," Mr. Rapallo replied.

"Before breakfast?" Tom inquired.

"Before daybreak!" his uncle answered; "that is to say, it ought to be light enough for us to work soon after four o'clock, as the sun rises at half-past four."

"Oh!" said Tom, feeling that here was an added new experience for him, as he had never in his life been out of the house before six o'clock in the morning.

"We must get our work done before anybody is stirring about," Mr. Rapallo explained. "That's our only chance of doing what we have to do without fear of interruption. We don't want to have a crowd about us when we are playing the hose on that pile of earth there; and I think that hydraulic mining in the streets of New York is novelty enough to draw a crowd pretty quickly, even in this part of the city. Fortunately, there is hardly a house near enough to the place where we are going to mine to make it likely that we shall disturb any one so early in the morning. Besides, we sha'n't make much noise."

"It's a good thing that there is n't a station of the elevated railroad on either of the streets that go past the place," Tom remarked. "There are people coming and going to the stations at all hours of the night, so Cissy tells me. His house is just by a station."

"I do not think any one is likely to see us at work unless he suspects what we are up to," said Uncle Dick. "By the way, is there any danger from that inquisitive boy you used to call Corkscrew?"

"No," Tom answered. "I don't believe Corkscrew Lott will be up at half-past four—or at half-past six either."

"I hope we shall have our job done before six," said Mr. Rapallo.

"Of course," Tom continued, "Corkscrew would get up over-night if he thought he could pry out anything. But I don't believe that he will bother us this time, because he is in bed with a sprained ankle."

"Then we need not worry about him," Uncle Dick remarked.

"I heard that he was better this morning," Tom added, doubtfully. "Perhaps he 'll be out by Decoration Day."

Mr. Rapallo replied: "I do not believe that there is much chance of this Corkscrew's bothering us; and if he does, why—there will be time enough to attend to him then."

And when the time came, Uncle Dick was able to attend to him.

On Monday, Tom told Cissy Smith and Harry Zachary that all was ready to begin work the next morning. Decoration Day came on a Tuesday that year.

"Shucks!" cried Cissy, "that lets me out. Pop will want to know where I'm going, if I try to get out of the house 'in the morning by the bright light,' as you want."

"And my mother would never let me go," said Harry Zachary; "at least not without asking awkward questions."

"I told Uncle Dick that I did n't believe you two fellows could get off; and he said he 'd settle that."

"Pop would settle me," Cissy declared, "if he caught me at it."

"Uncle Dick is going to ask Dr. Smith if you can't spend to-night with me so that we can all go off on an expedition with him in the morning."

"Then I guess it 'll be all right," Cissy admitted. "My father sets store by your uncle. He knew him out in Denver, you know, and he thinks a lot of him."

"And how about me?" asked Harry Zachary.

"Uncle Dick 's fixed that too," Tom explained. "He 's going to get my mother to write to your mother inviting you over to our house to spend the night with me."

"I reckon that 'll do it," responded Harry.

"Uncle Dick 's going to take Cissy into his room; and you are to sleep with me, Harry," said Tom.

"I don't believe we shall sleep much," Cissy declared; "we shall be too excited to sleep."

"Napoleon used to slumber soundly before his biggest and bloodiest battles," Harry Zachary remarked, reflectively; "and I reckon it's a good habit to get into."

As it happened, the boys went to bed far earlier than they had expected. Mr. Rapallo succeeded in arranging with Dr. Smith that Cissy should be left in his charge for one night, and Mrs. Zachary intrusted her son to Mrs. Paulding—to whom Uncle Dick gave no reason for the invitation other than that he was going to take the three boys out, and that they would see the sun rise.

When Polly heard this, she wanted to go, too. But Mr. Rapallo tactfully suggested a variety of reasons why she should not join the party; and some one of them must have struck the little girl as adequate, for she did not renew her request.

After supper—during which meal it had been very difficult for the three boys to refrain from discussing the subject they were all thinking about—Mr. Rapallo gave them each a coil of hose, and they set out for the vacant block. There was more hose than could conveniently be carried at once by the four of them. So they took about half of it the evening before and left it in the open air, half-hidden under the bushes. There was no moon, and Mr. Rapallo thought that it would be perfectly safe to trust the hose at night in a place where nobody was likely to go.

When they had returned to the house it was barely eight

"THUS THE PROCESSION SET OUT."

o'clock, but Uncle Dick promptly sent the boys off to bed; — or rather, he led the way himself, answering their protests by the assertion that they would need all the sleep they could get. He declared that he was not going to have his workmen too sleepy to see what they were about in the morning.

He set them the example himself, and all four were sound asleep before nine o'clock.

They had had nearly seven hours' slumber when Mr. Rapallo roused them. In the gray dawn — which struck them as being colder and darker than they had expected — the boys dressed themselves hastily. They gladly ate the bread and butter that Uncle Dick had ready for them, and each drank a glass or two of milk.

Then they crept softly downstairs and out into the garden. Mr. Rapallo divided the rest of the hose among them, and added to his own load three light spades and a pickax.

Thus the procession set out. Tom's heart had already begun to beat with alternating hopes and doubts; he was in haste to get at the work and to find the buried treasure as soon as might be. Cissy Smith and Harry Zachary had a boyish delight in the pleasantly romantic flavor of the adventure. To them it was as if they were knights-errant going to a rescue, or scouts setting out on a scalp-hunt, or, perhaps, pirates making ready for a sea-fight against a Spanish galleon laden with doubloons. Harry Zachary's imagination was the more active; but in his own way Cissy Smith took quite as much enjoyment in the situation.

CHAPTER XIX.

JEFFREY KERR'S BOOTY.

THEY walked on as the gray dawn was breaking with a faint, rosy tinge in the eastern sky. Two abreast, they bore with them the implements of their new craft Tied in a bundle and slung over his shoulder, Tom had also the bags in which to put the buried treasure.

When they had come to the vacant block they set down part of the hose on the sidewalk. The rest they carried with them down the steep sides of the parallelogram.

The first thing Tom and Mr. Rapallo did was to make sure that the things which had been brought over-night were still there. Apparently no one had touched these.

"Now, boys," cried Uncle Dick, "I'll go to work and get the hose ready, while you dig me a trench to carry off the water and the waste it will wash down."

The stepping-stones crossed what had been the middle of a wide pool into which the brook had broadened. A little below, the ground sloped away sharply. As Tom believed that the body of Jeffrey Kerr lay at the bottom of the pool, covered with sand, it was needful to remove not only the later rubbish, shot down from the street when the projecting tongue of land was made out into the block, but also to get a fall of water sufficient to carry off the sand at the bottom of the pool.

Fortunately, this was not a difficult task. By digging a trench a foot wide around a rock which had retarded the stream, and by carrying it along less than twenty feet, the natural declivity of the ground would then bear the water off to the open culvert at the end of the block.

Mr. Rapallo consulted with the boys as to the best course of this little trench. Then he roughly traced its path with the point of the pick, loosening the earth here and there where it seemed more than ordinarily compact. They set to work with the spades he had brought, while he went over to make ready the hose. The sections of common kind were first unrolled and stretched out across the block from the hydrant toward the point of attack. He screwed them firmly together. Then he went up to the hydrant and fastened to it the section of heavier hose, to the lower end of which was affixed a screw-joint to receive the end of the garden hose. By the aid of this, Mr. Rapallo joined the two kinds; and he had then a flexible tube more than a hundred and fifty feet long, with the hydrant at one end and a broad nozle at the other.

When he had thus prepared the hose for its work, he went over to the trench to see how the boys were getting on.

By this time the sun had risen and was visible, a dull red ball glowing in the east and slowly climbing the sky.

"Are you all ready?" cried Tom, as his uncle came up.

"I can turn on the water now if you have the trench done," was the answer.

The boys had followed the line Mr. Rapallo had traced, and, working with the eagerness and enthusiastic strength of youth, they had dug a ditch both broader and deeper than he had declared to be necessary.

"That's excellent," said Uncle Dick, when he saw what they had done. "It could n't be better."

"Shall we knock off now?" asked Cissy.

"You need n't do anything more to the trench," Mr. Rapallo answered. "That is just right. Gather up the spades and take them back out of the way of the water."

Then as they drew back he explained what he proposed next. What they needed to do was to lay bare the original surface of the pool by the stepping-stones. To do that they would have to wash out a hole in the bank at least twenty feet broad, perhaps fifteen high, and certainly ten feet deep.

"Can you do that with the hose?" asked Cissy, doubtfully.

"I think so," Mr. Rapallo answered. "Luckily, we shall have a strong head of water. Owing to the work on the new aqueduct, part of the supply for this portion of the city has been shut off below us for three or four days, so that hereabout there is a very full pressure. What I 'm most in doubt about is whether this small hose will stand it. We might as well find out as soon as possible. Tom, you can take this key and turn on the hydrant up there."

Tom hastily grasped the key, and sprang away across the open space. In a minute he had climbed to the street and turned on the water.

Mr. Rapallo seized the hose by the long brass nozle and stood pointing it firmly toward the bank of earth before him. As Tom opened the valve of the hydrant, the long line of hose stiffened and filled out. There was a whishing of air out of the nozle as the water rushed into the flexible tube. At the juncture of the larger hose with the smaller the joint was not tight, and a fine spray filled the air.

"Let's see if you can tighten that," cried Mr. Rapallo to Cissy, who ran back at once and succeeded in stopping the leak.

Then the smaller hose distended to the utmost. But Mr. Rapallo's fears were nearly groundless, for it was stanch and stood the strain.

It seemed but a second after Tom had turned the handle of the hydrant that a stout stream of water gushed solidly from the end of the pipe and curved in a powerful arch toward the bank before them.

Uncle Dick turned the stream upon the lower end of the trench the boys had dug, and in a minute he had washed it out to double its former capacity.

On his way back Tom joined Cissy and assisted him to tighten the valve which united the two kinds of hose. Harry Zachary had been helping Mr. Rapallo to get the end of the tube into working order, adjusting the curves and straightening it, so that the utmost force of the water might be available.

When he had washed out the trench, Mr. Rapallo raised the nozle carefully and directed the stream full at the center of the bank before him, striking it at what had been the level of the ground before the filling-in. The water plunged into the soft earth, and in less than five minutes it had washed out a large cave five or six feet deep.

Then Uncle Dick brought the force of the current again into the ditch, which had partly filled up. The stream, adroitly applied first at the lower end, swept out the trench as if a giant were at work on it with a huge broom.

Turning the water again on the bank of earth, Mr. Rapallo loosened the overhanging roof of the cavern he had first made, and it fell in soft heaps as the stream bored its way into the mound of earth. The hose removed the dirt faster than a dozen men could have shoveled it away; and a little attention now and then served to spread the stuff washed out over the lower part of the vacant block, leaving open a channel by which the water could make its escape to the culvert.

Minute by minute the cavity in the tongue of made land grew larger and larger, and the rubbish dumped there — ashes, builder's dirt, even old bits of brick and odds and ends of broken plaster — seemed to melt away under the impact of the curving current of water.

The sun slowly rose, and its early rays fell on this bending fountain, which sparkled as if it were a string of diamonds. As yet not a single passer-by had disturbed them at their work. But now and again the rattle of an early milk-cart could be heard in the morning quiet.

Once, when the bulk of the earth to be removed was nearly gone, Harry Zachary tapped Mr. Rapallo on the shoulder and pointed to the avenue on the west of them. Uncle Dick turned off the flow at once, and in the silence they heard the wagon of a market-gardener come rumbling toward them. Mr. Rapallo raised his hand and they all sheltered themselves hastily under the shadow of the bank until the intruder had passed on out of hearing.

As Uncle Dick turned on the water again he said, "We've been very lucky, so far. But as soon as we get this first job done I think we had better put out sentinels."

In a few minutes more the heap of dirt was washed away and the original level of the ground was laid bare up to the edge of the tall rock by the side of which Tom hoped to find his great-grandfather's guineas.

Uncle Dick thoroughly cleaned out the trench again and then turned off the stream.

"Now, Tom," he said, "here we've got down to the surface of the soil as it used to be. We are now standing on what was the bottom of the brook before it dried up. Where had we best begin on this?"

"Here," Tom answered, pointing to the base of the tall rock. "At least it seems to me that if a man tried to cross on those stepping-stones there, and got washed off by the brook, his body would be carried into the pool there, and then rolled over and over and nearer and nearer to that rock."

"Well," Uncle Dick returned, "I think that's the place, myself. But we must clear away here so that the water can get in its fine work."

He took the pickax and loosened a few stones and pried them out. The boys opened another trench leading down to the first ditch.

When this was done, Mr. Rapallo said, "We shall know in ten minutes now whether Tom has located his mine properly, or whether the claim is to be abandoned."

Tom was excited, and his voice shook as he answered, "Go ahead, Uncle Dick; the sooner I know the better."

"I think we ought to have outposts," Mr. Rapallo declared "Cissy, will you keep your eyes open for any one approaching from the south or east? Harry, you take charge of the north side and the west. Tom, stay with me."

This last admonition was hardly necessary, as it would have been difficult to make Tom move a step just then.

Cissy went back to the left of the group and looked about him. Harry withdrew a little to the right. But the fascination of expectancy was upon them both, and they kept a most negligent watch. They had eyes only for the stream of water, as Mr. Rapallo turned it on again and as it tore its way into the compact sand which had formed the bottom of the brook. Only now and then did they recall their appointed duties, and then they would give but a hasty glance around.

The water washed out the edge of the bottom of the pool, and Mr. Rapallo was able to expose a depth of fully five feet, into which the stream was steadily eating its way. As the open space approached nearer and nearer to the tall rock at the base of which Tom hoped to find the buried treasure, his heart began to beat, and he pressed forward in his eagerness to be the first to see whatever might have been hidden in the sand of the brook.

When about two yards only remained between the tall rock and the widening breach made by the water, he thought he caught sight of something white. With a cry he sprang forward, and the stream of water washed away the sand which had concealed the bones of a human foot and leg.

At that moment there came a whistle from Cissy Smith:

In a second, as it seemed, this was followed by a second warning from Harry Zachary:

Involuntarily, Tom whistled the answer:

Then he looked at Cissy, who was pointing to the figure of a man standing on the sidewalk behind them, within a yard of the hydrant.

Mr. Rapallo looked also, and then waved his hand. The man waved back.

"That's all right," said Uncle Dick.

Something in the man's gesture seemed familiar to Tom

"IN A SECOND HE WAS SOAKED THROUGH."

as he saw it indistinctly in the growing light of the morning.

"Is n't that the Old Gentleman who leaned over the Wall?" he asked.

"Yes," his uncle replied. "And is n't that your friend Corkscrew?" he continued, indicating a tall figure in high boots who was then advancing out on the tongue of made land before them.

This was the stranger Harry Zachary had seen when it

was too late. As this visitor came to the edge of the hollow which they had washed out, they knew that it was Corkscrew Lott.

"What's he doing here?" Tom wondered. "I thought he was in bed with a sprained foot."

"I'll send him to bed again with a shock of surprise," said Mr. Rapallo, raising the nozle again and turning on the stream.

As it gushed forth Uncle Dick aimed it full and square at Corkscrew, and it took the intruder first in the chest and then in the face. In a second he was soaked through. He turned and twisted and staggered back, but Mr. Rapallo never relented. The full stream was kept steadily on the inquisitive visitor until the tall boy crawled out on the sidewalk and started home on a full run.

As soon as he was out of sight, Tom cried to Mr. Rapallo, "Turn it on the place where it was before, Uncle Dick; I think I saw a bone there!"

"I thought so, too," Mr. Rapallo replied, as the full head of water began searching again in the sand.

Tom ran forward as far as he could, and in a moment he gave a cry of joy; for the water was uncovering a human skeleton, and among the bones he had caught a glitter of gold.

CHAPTER XX.

THE "WORKING HYPOTHESIS."

R. RAPALLO instantly turned the valve in the nozle of the tube and shut off the water. He threw down the hose and sprang forward to see what had been discovered.

There in the sand were the lower bones of a human skeleton, bleached white by time. The feet were already separated by the action of the water, and the shin-bones were detached at the knees.

The three boys stood by the side of Mr. Rapallo, looking with intense interest at these relics of what had once been a fellow human-being. Amid the sand, and by the side of a thigh-bone half uncovered by the stream of water, lay a dozen or more yellow coins.

Tom Paulding came closer, stooped and picked these out. They were dull, most of them, from their long burial in the earth, and some of them were covered with mold or incrusted with rusty earth. But one had been protected, perhaps by its position in the center of the bag; and this one glittered as the early rays of the sun fell on it.

"TOM PAULDING STOOPED AND PICKED OUT A DOZEN YELLOW COINS."

The boy held it out to Mr. Rapallo. "This is a guinea, Uncle Dick. I have seen pictures of them," he cried. "And see, the portrait of Georgius III."

Mr. Rapallo took the coin and looked at it carefully, turning it over. "It seems a little queer somehow," he remarked, "but it is a George the Third guinea. There can be no doubt of that."

"Then my guess was right," Tom said; "and we have found Jeffrey Kerr."

"The 'working hypothesis' worked excellently," his uncle answered. "This must be the skeleton of Jeffrey Kerr, and these are the guineas he stole. The punishment followed hard on the crime; and it was the weight of the stolen money which caused his death here at the bottom of the pool a few minutes after the theft, and when it seemed as if he had made his escape and got off scot-free. The retribution was swift enough for once; and the manner of it worked out a singular case of poetic justice."

"These six or seven coins are not all the money, I suppose?" asked Cissy.

"Of course not," Tom declared; "there are two thousand of them in all. We shall find them safe enough now."

"Shall I play the hose for you?" Harry Zachary inquired.

"No," Mr. Rapallo answered. "I think we must abandon our hydraulic mining now. I'm afraid the force of the stream of water might wash away the coins before we could get at them. We have found the gold now, and we had best dig it out carefully ourselves."

He himself took the pickax, and gently loosened all the earth about the upper part of the skeleton, which was not as yet uncovered. Then, with the spades, the boys very cautiously removed the sand from about the bones of the dead man's body. Every spadeful taken away was sifted through their fingers, and a little pile of guineas began to heap up near the skull, where Tom had laid the bags he had brought to carry home the treasure when he should find it. The stolen money had been tied in four bags originally; and they discovered the coins in four separate heaps, but they had been slightly scattered in the century and more between the loss of the guineas by Nicholas Paulding and their recovery by his great-grandson.

Two of these little heaps of coins were close together under the thighs of the skeleton; and it was from one of these heaps that the first glittering guinea had been washed out.

"Uncle Dick," said Tom, as they picked up these coins and put them in the bags, "do you remember that one of the papers I showed you said that Jeffrey Kerr had on a big overcoat with pockets?"

"Yes," Mr. Rapallo answered; "what of it?"

"Well," returned Tom, "I should n't wonder if these two piles of gold here under the body were once in the two of the bags which he had put into the pockets of his coat."

"I see," Mr. Rapallo responded; "and you think these pockets it was that weighted him down when he struggled for life in the swift waters of the swollen brook? I think it very likely."

The two other heaps were not so near together. The bags containing the coins in these piles had apparently been held in his hands until the thief fell into the stream as he was crossing the stepping-stones. With an involuntary clutch he had carried them with him as he went down into the pool. Perhaps he had then released them in his efforts to get free, perhaps they also had been attached to his person.

"It may be that the man did not make any struggle at all," said Mr. Rapallo, as they discussed these queries while gathering the coins together and putting them in the new bags. "He was fired on twice, remember; and at the second shot the sentry heard a cry of pain. Now it may be that he was wounded and faint, and so had no strength left."

"I wonder—" Harry Zachary remarked, as he went up to the bones and began to examine them carefully. "I reckon you're right, Mr. Rapallo," he cried a minute later. "That second shot took him in the shoulder."

"How do you know?" asked Cissy Smith, skeptically.

"Here's the hole in the bone," Harry answered; "and here is the bullet that made it." And with that he pulled out a large leaden ball that had been fast to the shoulder-blade.

"Then there can be no doubt now," said Mr. Rapallo, "as to the identity of the skeleton before us, as to the cause of his death, and as to the ownership of this gold. The more we discover about this, the more closely does everything fit together in accordance with Tom's 'working hypothesis.'"

When they had picked up the last coin in the four heaps, and after they had searched the sand below and on all sides without finding a single separate guinea, Mr. Rapallo said at last, "I think our work is done. There is no use in our lingering here and looking for more."

"There have been three more carts along here in the last ten minutes," Cissy remarked; "and I think it is about time for us to light out, if we don't want a crowd about us."

"That's so," Tom replied. "There may be a dozen people down here before we know it."

"Very well," Mr. Rapallo responded; "we may get away at once. But first let us at least give these poor bones a decent burial-place. They belonged to a thief who died almost in the act of stealing; but he was our fellow-man, after all, and we must do by him as we may hope to be done by."

Tom dug a light trench in the sand almost exactly where they had first seen the skeleton, and Harry Zachary gathered the bones together and placed them reverently in the grave. Then Cissy and Tom shoveled sand over the skeleton, hiding it from all prying eyes and heaping over it a mound, like those seen in cemeteries.

When this was done decently and in order, Mr. Rapallo bade the boys collect the spades and the pickax. He went back to the hydrant and turned off the water. Then he took off the hose and threw it over into the vacant block. Joining the boys again, he unfastened the section of the hose to which the nozle was attached, and this he coiled up to take away with him.

"We'll come back for the rest of the hose when it is dark,"

he explained. "For the present, we'll leave it here. I doubt whether anybody will notice it."

Then they took up their march homeward. Tom Paulding carried two bags of the recovered guineas, but his heart was so light that it seemed to him as if three times their weight would be no burden. Cissy Smith and Harry Zachary had each one of the other two bags. The boys also divided between them the pickax and the spades, as Mr. Rapallo was heavily laden with a coil of hose.

They had kept no count of time while they had been at work, and the hours had passed over them unperceived. The sun now rode high on the horizon. The roar of the great city rose on the air, only a little less resounding because the day was a holiday. The rattle of carts in the neighboring streets was frequent, so was the rolling of the trains on the elevated railroad. The city was awake again, and it was making ready to honor the dead heroes of the war, and to deck their graves with green garlands and with the bright flowers of the spring-time.

"If you don't mind, Tom," said Harry Zachary, as they walked side by side, "I'd like to keep the bullet."

"What bullet?" asked Tom, in surprise.

"The ball I found in the dead man's shoulder," Harry explained.

"But it does n't belong to me," Tom declared. "You found it. I suppose you 've a right to it."

"I want to keep it," Harry responded; "it 's a curious thing to have in the house; and I reckon it 's a talisman."

"A talisman?" repeated Tom.

"Yes," Harry answered, "like those they have in the old stories—something that will defend you from evil and bring you luck."

"Shucks!" said Cissy Smith, forcibly. "Why should that old bullet bring you any more luck than it brought Jeffrey Kerr? And it brought him to the bottom of the creek, and it left him there."

"I can keep it if I want it, I reckon," Harry remarked, placidly.

"Uncle Dick," Tom asked, "was n't that the Old Gentleman who leaned over the Wall—the man who stood by the hydrant just as we found the gold?"

"Yes," Mr. Rapallo answered; "that was Joshua Hoffmann."

"I did n't see him go away," Tom continued. "I wonder how long he stayed there."

"I 'd like to know how he came to be there at all," cried Cissy Smith.

"That 's so," Tom declared. "How did he know what we were going to do?"

Mr. Rapallo did not answer this direct question. Indeed, he parried it by another.

"How did your friend Corkscrew happen to get up so early?" he asked.

"I guess he won't feel encouraged to try it again," said Cissy. "You soused him well! Oh, how he did twist and squirm when you turned the hose full on him!

It was more fun than the circus." And Cissy laughed heartily at the recollection of Corkscrew's ludicrous appearance.

So did the other boys; and Mr. Rapallo joined in their merriment.

"He did look a little surprised," said Uncle Dick. "I don't believe he had expected quite so cold a welcome."

"If Corkscrew had only sprained his tongue instead of his foot," suggested Cissy, "so that he could n't ask any more questions, it would be money in his pocket."

"I 'd like to ask a question myself," Tom declared. "I 'd like to know how Corkscrew got news of our enterprise. I did n't tell him."

There was a guilty silence on the part of Harry Zachary, as if he thought that possibly something he might have hinted had been sufficient to bring Lott out of his bed at daybreak, in the hope of finding out something he was not meant to know.

By this time they had come to the flight of wooden steps which led from the sidewalk to the knob of sand on which stood Mrs. Paulding's house.

"Now, boys," said Mr. Rapallo, "I have to thank you for the assistance you have been to us—"

"Yes," almost interrupted Tom, "I 'm ever so much obliged to you both."

"I don't know what we should have done without your aid," Mr. Rapallo continued.

"Oh, that 's nothing," said Cissy Smith.

"We'd do twice as much if we could," said Harry Zachary.

"Now I've got to ask one more favor," Mr. Rapallo went on. "I want you to promise me one thing."

"We'll promise," replied Cissy.

"Of course," declared Harry.

"I want you to promise me," said Uncle Dick, "not to tell anybody about this morning's work."

"What?" cried Cissy, "not tell anybody?"

"Not ever tell?" Harry asked.

It was obvious that both lads were grievously disappointed, as they had hoped to set forth the whole story to all their friends, with every interesting detail. Very few boys in New York ever had a hand in the recovery of buried treasure; if they had to keep their share secret, Cissy and Harry both felt that they were deprived of the advantage of the unusual situation.

"Not for the present," Mr. Rapallo said. "Of course I know you will want to describe everything to your parents; and so you shall. But not to-day."

"To-morrow, then?" asked Harry.

"Perhaps you may tell to-morrow," Mr. Rapallo replied. "It is for the present only that I ask for secrecy. As soon as I can release you from the promise, I will."

"Oh, very well," said Cissy, frankly; "I'll promise."

"So will I," said Harry, with a sigh.

"If you are asked about anything, you can say that what you did is Tom Paulding's secret, and that you have promised to keep it solemnly," suggested Uncle Dick.

"So we can," Harry responded; "and I reckon that will make them want to know all the more."

His friends handed Tom the two bags of the recovered coins, and Mr. Rapallo relieved them of the spades. Then Cissy Smith and Harry Zachary departed.

When Tom and Uncle Dick stood at the top of the little flight of stairs, they saw Pauline come flying out of the house toward them.

"Remember, Tom," said his uncle, "you must not tell what you have been doing — at least, not yet."

"I know that," Tom responded.

"Where have you two boys been?" asked Polly.

"We've 'been to London to see the queen,'" replied Mr. Rapallo, gravely.

"And what have you got in those bags? — those are the ones I made for Tom, I'm sure."

Tom looked at his uncle, and made no answer.

"That's a secret," said Uncle Dick, laughing lightly as they went up the walk to the house.

"But I'm so good," cried the coaxing Pauline. "I'm so good you ought to tell me everything."

Tom and Mr. Rapallo were able to resist her blandishments, and the curiosity of Pauline was not satisfied that day.

CHAPTER XXI.

A STARTLING DISCOVERY.

AULINE followed her uncle and her brother rather despondently to the door of the house.

"You need n't tell me anything if you don't want to," she said; "but I 'm good, and I 'll tell you something—and it 's something you 'll be glad to know, too. Breakfast is ready!"

And with that Parthian shaft of magnanimous reproach, she sped past them into the house.

"We had best get rid of the dirt before we go to table," Mr. Rapallo suggested.

"Hydraulic mining is a pretty wet thing to do," Tom declared. "I don't believe I 've got a dry rag on me; and there 's sand in my shoes and in my hair and in my ears."

They went upstairs, and Tom hid the four precious bags under the pillow of his bed; and then he made himself presentable for the breakfast-table.

He and his uncle had agreed that, if they succeeded in finding the treasure, they should keep it a secret until they had sold the gold and with the proceeds paid off the mortgage that worried Mrs. Paulding. Mr. Rapallo had explained to Tom that as the mortgagee had requested payment of the bond there probably would need to be no delay whatever. They might go down-town the next morning, sell the gold and pay the mortgage off, all in two hours.

Then Tom counted on the pleasure of going to his mother with the canceled bond and mortgage, and making her a present of it. In imagination he had gone over the scene half a dozen times; and he longed for the flash of joy which would surely pass over Mrs. Paulding's face.

Yet when Tom and his uncle came down to breakfast that Decoration Day morning, the temptation to tell his mother the whole story was almost more than the boy could resist.

Mrs. Paulding saw that something had happened, and that her son was in an unusual state of suppressed excitement. But she would not ask for any specific explanation, knowing that Tom had had Cissy and Harry in the house all night, and that the three boys had gone out early with Mr. Rapallo. To this daybreak excursion with her brother she ascribed all her son's excitement, and she wondered a little what they had been doing to cause it. But she had perfect confidence in her brother and in her son, and she knew that the latter would surely wish her to share in any pleasure he had enjoyed; so she asked no questions, content to be told whenever Tom was ready to tell her, and unwilling to mar his delight in the telling by any obtrusive inquiries.

Pauline was less reticent. At least, she had less self-control.

"Tom Paulding!" she exclaimed, as her brother took his seat at the table, "what is the matter with you this morning? And where have you been? You are just bursting with something to tell, and yet you won't let me know what it is."

"So you think Tom has something on his mind?" asked Mr. Rapallo.

"Indeed I do," she answered. "Do you know what it is?"

"Yes," replied her uncle.

"And will you tell me?" she begged. "Remember that I'm your only niece, and I'm so good."

"Oh, yes, I'll tell you what Tom has on his mind, if you want to know," said Mr. Rapallo.

Tom looked up at his uncle in surprise, but he caught the twinkle in Mr. Rapallo's eye, and he was reassured.

"Well, what is it?" Polly demanded. "Tell me quickly."

"It is a secret!" Mr. Rapallo answered solemnly.

"Oh, I know that," returned Polly, disappointed.

"Then I need not have told you," said her uncle.

"You have n't told me anything really," the little girl continued. "At least, you have n't told me what the secret is."

"If I told you that," Mr. Rapallo declared, with great gravity, "it would not be a secret any more,—so it would be no use to you."

"Oh!" cried Polly, "I never had an uncle as aggravoking as you are."

"Still, if you will conquer your just resentment," Mr. Rapallo went on, "and pass me my cup of tea, I shall take it as a favor and seek for an occasion to do as much for you."

A STARTLING DISCOVERY.

"Uncle Dick," said Pauline, "you are a goose!"

"Pauline!" called Mrs. Paulding, reprovingly.

"Oh, well, Uncle Dick knows what I mean," the little girl explained.

"I deny that I am a goose," said Mr. Rapallo; "but I will admit that Tom and I have been out this morning on a wild-goose chase."

"Did you get any?" asked Pauline.

"We got one," Mr. Rapallo replied; "it was a goose with golden eggs."

"But that's only a story," said the little girl, doubtfully.

"This was only a story;" her uncle answered, "but it came true."

"I don't think it's at all nice of you to puzzle me like this, Uncle Dick," Pauline declared, as she took Mr. Rapallo's teacup from her mother's hands and passed it to her uncle.

"Thank your ladyship," said Mr. Rapallo.

"Oh," cried Polly, suddenly, "you are going to see two girls!"

"Am I?" asked her uncle. "How do you know?"

"That's what Katie always says when she finds two tea-leaves floating in the cup," Pauline explained.

"Ah," exclaimed Mr. Rapallo, "so two leaves in my cup mean that I am to see two girls? And if they had been in your cup—"

"Then that would mean two boys," Polly broke in. "Of course, I don't believe it at all, but that's what Katie says. She believes all sorts of things."

"And where is the Brilliant Conversationalist this morning?" asked Mr. Rapallo.

"I think I heard the postman's whistle a minute ago," Mrs. Paulding answered; "she has probably gone out for the letters."

The Brilliant Conversationalist came in just then, with two letters in her hand. One she gave Mrs. Paulding, and the other she placed before Mr. Rapallo.

"There's only one for you, Mr. Richard," she said, with kindly interest. "Ye don't be gettin' as many as ye did."

"I'm in luck to-day as well as you, Tom," said Mr. Rapallo, when he had glanced over his letter, which he then folded up and put in his pocket without further remark.

"How is Tom in luck to-day?" asked Polly.

"That is part of the secret," answered her uncle.

"I don't like secrets," she replied, haughtily. "And I'm going to have some of my own," she added, hastily, "just to tease you."

Mr. Rapallo laughed at this inconsistent threat. Tom silently went on with his breakfast, scarcely trusting himself to speak, for fear that he might say more than he meant.

Mrs. Paulding had been reading her letter; and now she laid it down with a sigh.

"It's about that mortgage, Richard," she said, with anxiety and weariness in her voice; "they want it paid as soon as I can pay it."

"Perhaps that will be sooner than you think, Mother," cried Tom, involuntarily.

A STARTLING DISCOVERY.

"I agree with Tom," exclaimed Mr. Rapallo, hastily breaking in. "You can never tell what may turn up. Perhaps there may be good fortune in store for you."

"I'm not much of a believer in luck," said Mrs. Paulding, sadly.

"But, Mother, I know —" began Tom, impulsively.

Again Mr. Rapallo interrupted him sharply. "Tom," he cried, "if you have finished your breakfast, we'll go upstairs. You may remember that we have something to do there."

"Now what can you have to do on Decoration Day morning, I'd like to know," Polly declared. "I think this keeping of secrets and making allusions and hints is just too annoying for anything."

"Uncle Dick is right," said Tom, rising from the table. "We have work to do to-day."

Then he went around to his mother and put his arm about her and kissed her. He patted Polly's curls as he passed out of the room, and she shook her head indignantly.

When they were upstairs Mr. Rapallo said to Tom, "You came pretty near giving yourself away, then."

"I know I did," Tom answered. "I could n't bear to see my mother worrying about money when I've got enough here to make her comfortable."

"How do you know?" asked Mr. Rapallo. "You have n't counted it yet."

"I'll do it now," Tom responded, and he took a bag from under his pillow and emptied it out on the bed. Then he rapidly counted the coins into little heaps of ten each. There were forty-nine of these in the first bag, and three pieces over.

"You have made a pretty even division among the bags, apparently," said Mr. Rapallo. "Two thousand guineas in four equal parts would be five hundred in each bag; and you have four hundred and ninety-three in that one."

"I'll count the others," Tom exclaimed, "and perhaps one of them has seven guineas more than its share."

"You must not expect to find every one of the two thousand guineas," Mr. Rapallo declared; "that would be a little too much. You must be satisfied if you have nineteen hundred or thereabouts. It is a mistake to be too grasping. I wonder if I am doing right myself, in trying for more than I can get now? You know that I have been at work on a little invention?—well, that letter I got this morning brought me a very good offer for all my rights in it."

"Are you going to take it?" asked Tom, as he ranged the contents of the second bag in little heaps of ten.

"I think not," his uncle answered. "I hope I can do better."

"There are five hundred and two in this bag," Tom declared.

"That is to say," Mr. Rapallo commented, "you have nine hundred and ninety-five in the two bags. At that rate you would be short only ten guineas in the two thousand."

And this was almost exactly as it turned out. The third bag contained four hundred and seventy-four, and the fourth had five hundred and eighteen. Thus in the four bags there were nineteen hundred and eighty-seven of the two thousand guineas stolen from Tom's great-grandfather. Only thirteen of them had been washed away or missed by the eager fingers of Tom and his friends.

"How much in our money will nineteen hundred and eighty-seven guineas be?" asked Tom.

"A little more than ten thousand dollars, I think," his uncle answered.

"Ten thousand dollars!" repeated the boy, awed by the amount.

"That is, if you get only the bullion value of the gold," continued Mr. Rapallo. "Perhaps some of the separate coins here may have a value of their own, from their rarity. There may be guineas of Queen Anne and of William and Mary. Some of them are perhaps worth two or three times their weight as mere specie."

As Mr. Rapallo was speaking, Tom was rapidly turning over the little heaps that had come out of the fourth bag, which was still on his bed.

"These are all George the Third," he said, "every one of them. There is n't a coin in this heap that has n't his head on it."

"That is curious," said his uncle.

"And these are all of the same year, too," cried Tom. "Seventeen hundred and seventy."

"That is rather remarkable," Mr. Rapallo declared; "but I suppose you have there the contents of one of the old bags which had been filled from a stock of coin received at one shipment from the mint in London."

"But the other bags are all the same," Tom returned, quickly examining the handful of coins he had taken from one of the other bags.

"They can't be all alike," Uncle Dick responded. "Two thousand guineas of the same mintage would be very unlikely to be paid out all at once six years after the date."

"I have n't found a single guinea of any year but seventeen seventy," said Tom, looking at coin after coin.

"That is certainly suspicious," Mr. Rapallo remarked.

"Suspicious?" echoed Tom.

"Oh!" cried Uncle Dick, starting up. "I hope not! And yet it would explain one thing."

"What is it?" Tom asked, with a first faint chill of doubt.

Mr. Rapallo did not answer. He went into his own room and came back at once, with a small stone in his hand and a glass bottle containing a colorless liquid.

Setting the bottle down on the table, he took at random a guinea from each of the four bags; and with each he made a mark on the stone, on the fine grain of which he rubbed off a bit of the soft metal. Then he put down the coins, and, taking up the glass stopper of the bottle, he touched a drop of the liquid to the four marks. They turned dark and disappeared. Mr. Rapallo sighed, and cast a glance of pity on his nephew.

Then he plunged his hand deep down into each of the four bags in turn and drew forth four more guineas, and tested these as he had tested the first four; and again the marks turned dark and disappeared.

"Uncle Dick, what are you doing?" cried Tom. "Is anything—"

"Tom," said Mr. Rapallo, placing his hand affectionately

"TAKING UP THE STOPPER, HE TOUCHED A DROP OF THE LIQUID TO THE MARKS."

on the boy's shoulder, "are you strong enough to learn the truth at once?"

"What do you mean?" Tom asked, rising involuntarily, with a sudden iciness of his hands and feet.

"I mean," his uncle answered, slowly, "that I am afraid

that all these guineas you have toiled for so bravely are counterfeit."

"Counterfeit?" repeated the boy.

"Yes," Mr. Rapallo replied; "I have tested eight of these coins taken at random, and no one of them is gold. I am afraid there is not a genuine guinea in all your two thousand here."

Tom said nothing for a minute or more. He drew a long breath and stared straight before him. He heard the wavering whistle of a river steamer; and then he caught the faint notes of a brass band leading a local post of the Grand Army of the Republic to take part in the procession of the day.

At last he looked up at his uncle, and said, "Poor mother! I've no surprise for her now."

CHAPTER XXII.

COUNSEL.

NCLE DICK laid his hand gently on Tom Paulding's shoulder.

"Brace up, my boy," said he, with sympathy in his voice. "You have met with a misfortune; and just now it seems to you as if the world was all hung with black, and life not worth living. Look up, and you will see that the sun is still shining outside. Live to be as old as I am, and you will learn to expect little and to be satisfied with less. In the meanwhile, keep a stout heart."

"I have thought about this so long, Uncle Dick," replied the boy; "I have n't thought of anything else for months now; and the money meant so much to us all — it 's hard to have to give it up all of a sudden, just when we 'd laid hands on it at last."

"I know," his uncle responded. "The blow is hard to bear at best, and you got it at the very moment when it was the hardest to stand. I see that, and I am heartily sorry for you. But you must not give up the struggle because you have lost the first skirmish."

"You are right, I know," Tom returned, sadly. "But I had so many good uses for those two thousand guineas. They would have paid off the mortgage and kept mother from worrying any more about that. Then I could have had an education, as my father had and my grandfather—they were both graduated from Columbia College, you know—and I wanted to work at the School of Mines. Now I shall have to go into a store; of course, I shall try and do my best there; but I don't believe that's what I can do best. I like out-doors, and the open air, and I used to see myself working hard in the mountains, planning a mine and looking after the work. Well," and he sighed again, "that's all over now," and as he said this there was a lump in his throat.

"Perhaps not," his uncle remarked, quietly.

"But you said this money is all counterfeit?" Tom returned.

"I think so," Uncle Dick declared.

"Well, then?" asked Tom.

"This is not all the money there is in the world," Mr. Rapallo replied, cheerfully, "nor have you no other chances but the one which has gone back on you this morning. Things are never as bad as we think they are at first."

"I think I *know* just how bad this thing is—for me," said the boy, gloomily.

"You valued the finding of this buried treasure," his uncle responded, "because of the uses you could put it to—the relief of your mother, your own education, certain advantages for your sister. Well, these are all things which may be obtained in other ways—perhaps not all at once, but in time."

"I don't see how," said Tom, doubtfully.

"Neither do I now," Mr. Rapallo replied; "if I did, I should show you at once. But you did not mean to keep your two thousand guineas as a miser's hoard to gloat over—"

"Of course I did n't," cried Tom, forcibly.

"As you intended to spend it to produce certain results," his uncle went on, "the loss of this money is the loss only of one of the means by which these results could be secured. There are other ways of accomplishing them. You and I must look them up. I am sure that we shall find something —even if it is not all we seek. You know that we make a mistake if we expect the millennium over-night; in my experience it rarely comes before the day after to-morrow."

Tom smiled faintly at this speech of his uncle's; and Mr. Rapallo, who had been waiting for this smile, held out his hand and gave the boy a hearty clasp.

"Now, do you remember, Tom," he asked, cheerily, as though determined not to be downcast, "that you once told me that there were two things that puzzled you when you had first gone through the box of papers?"

"Yes," answered his nephew. "First, I wanted to know where the money was; and second, I wondered why my grandfather had given over the search so suddenly, as it seemed."

"We have solved both problems, I think, by this morning's work," Mr. Rapallo remarked. "You found the money as you had hoped, that was one thing; and then you found that it was counterfeit, and perhaps that was the reason of the other."

"Do you think my grandfather knew that the two thousand guineas were not really gold?" asked Tom.

"Yes," answered his uncle.

"And that *that* was the reason why he gave over the search all at once?" Tom pursued.

"Yes," said Uncle Dick for the second time.

"But how could he know that?" cried the boy. "We did n't find it out till we had found the money, and we know he did n't find the money."

"Then he must have made the discovery in some other way," declared Uncle Dick. "From whom did your great-grandfather get the two thousand guineas?"

"From a man named Simon Horwitz," answered Tom. Then suddenly he cried, "Oh!"

"Well?" said his uncle.

"Well, I think you must be right," the boy explained. "My grandfather must have been told of the fraud, and that the buried treasure was n't worth bothering about. And the way he knew this was, somehow, from the only man who knew about the cheat."

"You mean Simon Horwitz?" asked Mr. Rapallo.

"I 'll show you in a minute," said Tom, as he pulled out the box of old papers and began to turn them over hastily in search of a particular paper. At last he found what he was seeking, and placed a folded piece of foolscap in his uncle's hands.

"There!" he said.

"This is indorsed 'Notes of Horwitz's Confession,' but there is nothing inside," Mr. Rapallo said, as he turned the paper over. "However, I think I see how it was. When your grandfather was collecting all possible information about the stolen guineas, he finally got from the man who had given his father the money a confession that it had been paid in counterfeit coin — that would account for the suspicious delay in its payment, too. Thereupon of course your grandfather ceased all effort to discover the whereabouts of the stolen money — which was really not money at all. He indorsed the cover of these 'Notes of Horwitz's Confession' and put it with the other papers, or thought he did. At all events, the cover of this confession is preserved with the other papers. And we find it too late, when we have had all our labor in vain."

"That would account for everything that used to puzzle me," Tom responded.

"Now, if I were you," said Mr. Rapallo, "I would go for your friends, Cissy Smith and Harry Zachary, and get them up here in this room; and I would tell them all about the counterfeit coin; and I would release them at once from their pledge of secrecy."

"Oh, Uncle Dick," cried Tom, "would you let them tell everybody?"

"Why not?" asked his uncle. "You cannot expect them to keep our morning's work a secret forever."

"I suppose not," said Tom, doubtfully.

"Well, then," Mr. Rapallo continued, "the sooner they get it over the better. Let them tell the whole story at once. And the final surprise about the counterfeit money will make the tale only the more interesting."

"That 's so," Tom assented, perceiving at once the force of this suggestion.

"You see, Tom," continued his uncle, "people generally will not know that you were going to do anything in particular with the money, and they will never suspect your great disappointment. Of course you need not tell anybody about that."

"Of course not," Tom declared, with undue emphasis.

"Except your mother," Mr. Rapallo added.

"Must she know?" asked Tom.

"Certainly," was the firm answer. "Go and tell her and Polly all about it at once. You may be sure that your mother will be glad to learn that you wanted the money to help her."

"I think she would have been pleased if we could have gone into her room and shown her the mortgage all paid off," said Tom, sighing again. "But there 's no use thinking of that now."

"I 've an appointment," Mr. Rapallo declared, looking at his watch, "or at least I am going to try to see a friend before he goes out. Will you come into your mother's room with me before I go?"

"Yes," Tom answered. "I may as well get it over as soon as I can."

Mr. Rapallo led the way to Mrs. Paulding's room, the door

of which stood wide open, as usual. Tom's mother was seated by the window, and by her side there was a basket of the household linen, which she was repairing. Pauline had a low chair by her mother's; and she was hemming towels.

"TOM TOLD HER THE WHOLE STORY."

"Just look at that hem, Uncle Dick!" cried Polly, as Mr. Rapallo entered the room. "I think it's as good, almost, as if it had been done on a machine."

"Is there any trouble?" asked Mrs. Paulding, reading the faces of her brother and her son.

"No," answered Mr. Rapallo. "There is no trouble of any kind, but Tom has had a sore disappointment, and I think it will do him good to tell you all about it."

Mrs. Paulding looked up, and Tom bent over and kissed her.

"Tom is a little crushed just now, Mary," Uncle Dick continued. "But he will get over it, and it won't hurt him. A boy is a little like a ball: you throw it down and it bounds up unhurt — that is, if it has any spring in it; and Tom has plenty of that."

When Mr. Rapallo had left them, Mrs. Paulding looked up at Tom again with a smile, and said, "Now, my boy, tell me all your trouble."

And Tom told her the whole story, his hopes, his expectations, his success, his disappointment. While he was telling it, his mother's quick sympathy sustained and cheered him. And when he had told her everything, he felt comforted, and the world was no longer hung with black.

CHAPTER XXIII.

CONCLUSION.

AFTER telling his mother and his sister the circumstances and the result of the quest which had occupied his mind for six months and more, Tom Paulding felt a little better. Already he was able to bear the poignant disappointment more bravely, and he tried to keep down the bitterness he had felt at first. By resolute determination he put away all repining, and so, as the day wore on, he began to pick up heart again.

In the afternoon he took Harry Zachary and Cissy Smith up into his own room, and he explained how it was that their labors were in vain. He showed them the counterfeit coins and repeated for them Mr. Rapallo's test with the touchstone.

"If we 'd only known," said Cissy, "that the gold we were after was n't gold at all, we would n't have been so keen after it, and we should n't have tried so hard to throw Corkscrew off the scent."

"I don't think I ever read of a buried treasure," remarked Harry, "that was n't real. It 's just as though the wicked magician had got hold of the secret talisman and had changed the coins from gold to dross."

"Shucks!" returned Cissy, forcibly; "the only wicked magician was that Simon Horwitz, and he 'd have to have had a talisman against old age and death, if he wanted to be alive now."

"Do you want us to keep this a secret any longer?" asked Harry, a little anxiously.

"No," Tom answered, "Uncle Dick says that the sooner it is known the sooner it will be forgotten."

"I don't want to forget it," was Cissy's reply. "I enjoyed all I had to do with it. And if it had been twice the trouble, I 'd have done it three times over, just for a sight of Corkscrew Lott twisting himself up into a double-bow knot when your uncle got the range on him!"

Even Tom was moved to laughter when he recalled the surprise expressed on Lott's face when he first received the full force of the stream of water.

At school the next day, when the news had spread, Tom was overwhelmed with questions of all sorts. Fortunately the comments of Corkscrew Lott were not made in Tom's hearing, or there might have been a renewal of the Battle of the Curls. Apparently Corkscrew remembered that decisive combat; and what he had to say about Tom Paulding's silly conduct was said behind Tom Paulding's back. No doubt this was wisest, for it is greatly to be feared that a fight would have been a great relief to Tom's feelings just then. Perhaps Corkscrew was shrewd enough to suspect this; at any rate, he kept out of Tom's way, and there was no overt act of hostility. Since the Battle of the Curls Corkscrew had continued to grow, and he was now nearly six feet high; he was by far the tallest boy in the school, and his long boots served to exaggerate his height; but Tom was in a frame of mind that would have made it dangerous for any one to have stood up before him in a fair fight.

At dinner that night Mr. Rapallo was late. He was a little quieter than usual, perhaps, and took pleasure in drawing Polly out and in getting her to talk about her school and her school friends.

The little girl mentioned that one of her friends was in bed with a bad attack of "new-mown hay."

Uncle Dick was puzzled. "I suppose you mean 'hay-fever,'" he said, "but this is not the season for it."

"It is n't 'hay-fever' at all," she declared, "it's new-mown hay; that's what the doctor called it."

"Oh!" and her uncle laughed out, "I see now. You mean pneumonia."

"That's just what I said," Polly asserted.

"Mary," said Mr. Rapallo, turning to Mrs. Paulding, "you do not know how happy I have been here with you; and I myself don't yet know how much I shall miss you all."

"You are not going away?" asked Mrs. Paulding.

"Again?" cried Polly; and you have only just come back."

Tom said nothing, but he looked at his uncle; and Mr. Rapallo knew by this glance how much his nephew would regret his departure.

"I am going away to-night," Uncle Dick declared.

"To-night?" echoed Polly.

"I hope you will not be gone so long as you were the last time," Mrs. Paulding exclaimed.

"I'm afraid I shall be gone longer," Mr. Rapallo answered. "In fact, I don't know when I shall be back. I'm a rolling stone, you see, and I am always rolling on and trying to gather moss. I leave New York to-night for San Francisco, and next week I expect to sail for Australia."

"But you won't stay there long?" Polly inquired.

"I doubt if I do," he answered; "for I have to go to Japan and China and India. And when I shall get back here again, I cannot venture even to guess—probably not for several years."

"Oh, Richard," said Mrs. Paulding, "I had hoped you would settle down here with us!"

"I hoped so, too," her brother replied, "but I'm a wanderer on the face of the earth, and there is no use in my trying to cast anchor anywhere. I've got to go out again into deep water now, and I suppose I may try to make myself believe that I start unwillingly; but I don't deceive myself. I'm getting restless again; I've seen the symptoms for some time; to-day the fever was at its height, so I took up with an offer Joshua Hoffmann made me, and I start off to-night."

"Then Marmee won't get her Chr—" Polly was going to finish with "—istmas present," when she remembered herself.

"Yes, she will," Uncle Dick remarked.

"I did n't say it out—not all of it," explained Pauline, blushing.

"And I did n't need you to remind me about it," her uncle responded, smiling.

Tom was sitting still, saying nothing, and thinking that his uncle's absence would leave a great void in the household, and almost wishing that he, too, might go to see these strange countries, Australia and India, China and Japan.

"When I went away at the beginning of the year," Mr. Rapallo continued, "I was working out a little invention I had to travel about here and there, investigating and improving my model. At last I completed it, and yesterday a man to whom I had shown it wrote and offered me a good price for it. I thought of refusing at first, but I went to see him yesterday afternoon, and we had a long talk, and finally I accepted the offer. This morning I received my money. It was a little more than I needed to pay off the mortgage on this house—"

"Richard!" cried Mrs. Paulding, her eyes filling with tears, while Tom's face flushed with sudden pleasure.

"And I thought that was the best thing I could do with the money," Mr. Rapallo went on; "so Mr. Duncan and I arranged with the lawyer of the mortgagee, and here is the document canceled. The first of June is a little late for a Christmas present, I know; but better late than never."

"I do not think I ought to let you give me this money of yours," said Mrs. Paulding.

"I do not think you can help yourself," answered her brother. "The deed is done—or at least the mortgage is, and that leaves the deed free. If Tom had had better luck with his hydraulic mining, I should n't have interfered with his intended arrangements, of course."

"I wanted to pay off the mortgage myself," said Tom, "but I'd rather have you do it than any one else; and of course I'm delighted that it is done. Mother won't worry now,— that was what I wanted most."

"I know that," his uncle replied, "but you want to go to the School of Mines also if you can, don't you?"

"Now with the mortgage no longer hanging over me, I think I can manage that," Mrs. Paulding declared.

"I think it can be arranged without any expense to you," Mr. Rapallo responded.

"How?" cried Tom. "I wish it could!"

"Well," Uncle Dick began, "I'll tell you how. Mr. Joshua Hoffmann—"

"That's the Old Gentleman who leaned over the Wall, is n't it?" asked Tom.

"The Old Gentleman who leaned over the Wall is Mr. Joshua Hoffmann," Mr. Rapallo replied. "He is an old friend of mine, and it is on his business that I am going to the East. One day when you passed us I told him about you, Tom,

MRS. PAULDING RECEIVES HER CHRISTMAS PRESENT.

and about your quest for buried treasure; and that is why he was standing by the hydrant yesterday morning when we were experimenting with the 'working hypothesis.' He was greatly interested in your success; he liked your hammering out your puzzle for yourself; and he was glad that you wanted a scientific education. When I told him about the unfortunate end of our wild-goose chase — how we had found a goose that laid eggs of imitation gold — he listened most attentively and with real sympathy. This morning he said to me, 'If that nephew of yours wants to come to me for the summer as a sort of private secretary — you say he writes a good hand — I'll take him with me on the *Rhadamanthus;* and if I find him to be what I think he is, I'll send him to the School of Mines at my own expense and give him a place at the Eldorado Works when he graduates. A boy with gumption and with grit — that's the kind of boy I like to have about me.'"

"Oh, Uncle!" cried Tom.

"Will you accept?" asked Mr. Rapallo.

"Won't I!" Tom returned. "That is, if mother can spare me this summer."

"I shall miss you, my boy, no doubt," Mrs. Paulding answered, "but of course you must go. The chance is too good to lose."

So it came to pass that Tom Paulding went on a quest for buried treasure; and found it; and it was worthless. He wanted the money for a double purpose; and these things came about in other ways. Yet his wild-goose chase had not been a piece of folly; he felt himself stronger for the striving, and perhaps he was stronger for the disappointment.

Whether his quest had been altogether a failure or not was a question Tom Paulding never solved. Sometimes it seemed to him that perhaps it may be a bad thing for a boy of New York at the end of the nineteenth century to expect to find buried treasure ready to his hand; the boy might just as well hope to have a fairy godmother. Now, we all know that fairy godmothers are very infrequent nowadays — in fact it may be said that they have gone quite out of fashion.

THE END.

14 DAY USE
RETURN TO DESK FROM WHICH BORROWED
LOAN DEPT.
This book is due on the last date stamped below, or on the date to which renewed.
Renewed books are subject to immediate recall.

14 Nov '59 CF	
REC'D LD	
OCT 31 1959	
FEB 5 1977	
REC. CIR. AUG 18 '78	

LD 21A–50m-4,'59
(A1724s10)476B

General Library
University of California
Berkeley

C030931670

www.ingramcontent.com/pod-product-compliance
Lightning Source LLC
Chambersburg PA
CBHW032139230426
43672CB00011B/2387